THE ALAMO

FOR THE TEXANS
WITH WHOM I'VE SOLDIERED
AND POUNDED TYPEWRITERS.

THE ALAMO

BY

JOHN MYERS MYERS

A BISON BOOK

UNIVERSITY OF NEBRASKA PRESS · LINCOLN

To—

JIM PUTNAM AND FRANK NAGY

*two men to like the tale
and maybe the telling*

CONTENTS

MAPS

THE ALAMO

FOREWORD

IN THE absence of footnotes it seems fitting to make a statement about the source material of the ensuing narrative.

Barring versions which may exist in manuscript, this is the first chronicle of the Alamo which seeks to present the story of that historic structure in full. Finding and assembling the necessary parts has been a fascinating but, at the same time, complicated business. Before they could be recognized with sureness, many of the scattered pieces were walked past time and again. Dozens upon dozens of those available were suspect upon discovery because mutually contradictory. The spurious could only be discarded with confidence after months of reviewing and collating.

It was at first surprising that information about so famous a fort should be hard to come by. In the light of actualities no surprise should have been felt. The truth is that the story of the Alamo is at once familiar to everybody and not known at all. The name has always been one to conjure with; but the name has belonged to a formless, if glorious, shade rather than to a solid body. Outside of Texas even contemporaries of the siege had little accurate information.

The few people who did know the story, or parts of it, at firsthand were not professional writers, and no enterprising historian sought them out. In the fashion of the day some of them wrote private journals, most of which have achieved circulation only in this century. The informative letters of certain ones have been preserved, while the pertinent statements of others have been passed down, not always in the form of direct quotations. Scholars like Yoakum and Bancroft have added to the sum of knowledge, but in the main it can be said that the facts have been saved in spite of histories rather than through their agency.

As the members of the Alamo garrison were killed to a man, a natural question is: Who then was qualified to write or speak authoritatively? The list begins with the dead warriors themselves, notably Travis, who sent out a number of letters containing details as to the progress of the siege. Then there were noncombatant and semi-noncombatant inmates of the fort who survived the event.

The number of these has not been computed to everyone's satisfaction, but there were a dozen more or less. Among those who left words for the record was the only American woman present, a Mrs. Almiram Dickenson, whose husband was an officer of the garrison. A Mrs. Horace Alsbury, who in spite of her name was a Mexican, also had something to say. She claimed to have been in the fort throughout the siege, whereas Mrs. Dickenson asserted that she was allowed to leave and take refuge with her fellow-countrymen two or three days before the end. Mrs. Dickinson also accused her of betraying the spent condition of the garrison to Santa Anna, although that could have been no more than an assumption on her part.

Joe, Travis' Negro body servant, apparently spared as an involuntary combatant—for he mentioned having a pistol— was interviewed by Houston and others a few days after the siege. There has been a tendency to put his statements aside, which seems unwarranted. He is described as intelligent, and he was there to see.

Of the children present, one called Jose Enriquez was eight at the time and was therefore able to recall certain things with tolerable clarity later on. His contribution was not large, but he did definitely remember that there was no such person within the walls of the Alamo as Madame Candelaria. For that reason, because of the absence of corroborative testimony, and because of the existence of quite a body of confuting evidence, the presence of the Candelaria woman is not acceptable.

In addition, there were actual members of the garrison who left before the final assault and thus were in a position to tell a portion of the story. Apparently between ten and fifteen couriers got through the Mexican lines at one stage or another of the combat. Regrettably, none of these left any written record of his own, but the statements of two were cited by people who later wrote them down. The ones referred to are Captain Juan Seguin, a Mexican officer of the Alamo garrison, and John W. Smith, who was in and out of the fort twice.

The only remaining garrison member who outlived the siege was Louis Rose, the French mercenary who deserted. He has generally been catalogued as a legend because his story didn't become common property until late in the nineteenth century. Recently, however, a scholar has unearthed a bundle of Texas court records for the years just following the siege. In not just one but in a number of cases relative to the disposal of property of men who had died in the Alamo, Rose's testimony was accepted as that of a man who had seen them in the fort not long before they were killed. With reservations, and allowing for the confessed coloration supplied by the man who finally wrote it down, his statement is admissible.

Civilian observation from without is represented by Francisco Ruiz, alcalde of San Antonio at the time and a man more or less friendly to both parties. As an official of a Mexican town his services were requisitioned by Santa Anna. In particular he was ordered, as he recorded, to have a group of citizens standing by to assist the wounded at the time of the final assault; and he was subsequently given the duty of segregating the bodies of the Alamo defenders from those of Mexican soldiers.

Mexican officers, including Santa Anna, wrote about the Alamo, but it should be noted that they did it under stress, after the Texas campaign was a failure. In general they weren't too concerned with facts. Their intent was primarily to salvage their damaged military reputations and secondarily to cut each other's throats politically. At various points their contradictory statements can profitably be checked against those of Sergeant Becera, an intelligent Mexican enlisted man, whose somewhat high-flown report also got on the record.

If the Mexican generals later wrote for their own benefit, their official orders are something else again; and a valuable document in the form of a diary was taken from Colonel Juan N. Almonte, Santa Anna's chief aide. His brief, daily notations make it possible to follow the siege from the attackers' viewpoint.

Then above and beyond the letters, quotations, memoirs, orders, manifestoes and depositions there was, as there nearly always is in such cases, a floating mass of details, the common knowledge of those intimate with the story at the time but attributable to no one in particular. Sometimes they turn up in a group, while at other times they are found loose, off by themselves. Many so dovetail with provable facts that they must be accepted; others have had to be rejected because they match with nothing.

Often indistinguishable from this class of data are the rumors which start almost simultaneously with the event, appearing as mysteriously as fruit flies when a bottle of wine is opened. In his maturity, for instance, one Texas memorialist confessed that as a youngster he invented a story of the last minutes of the Alamo to impress some greenhorns from the States. He hadn't expected to be taken seriously by anyone else and was confounded to discover that his version was being generally accepted as fact. The story he invented was that there were five last survivors of the garrison, of whom David Crockett was one, who surrendered on honorable terms, only to be murdered. That tale, fabricated within ten days of the fall of the Alamo, is now cited in encyclopedias and dictionaries.

Much confusion would have been avoided had there been an effort to investigate on the part of competent newspapermen, but there was none. The early reports, including those prepared by historians, were a jumble of facts, rumors and guesswork. Yoakum found out much of the story, but he came along a couple of decades later when many of the parts had already been buried in letters and diaries relegated to the attic. And in any case a man writing the history of a state could affort to devote so much space and no more to a single incident, however important.

The first to publish a separate account of the siege of the Alamo based on personal investigation didn't do so until 1860. This was Captain Reuben Marmaduke Potter, who revamped his pamphlet some years later. The captain had just about the neatest reportorial style since Caesar wrote about Gaul, but he confessedly often had to substitute "military probabilities" for facts in drawing his conclusions.

The captain's second and much improved version wasn't published until 1904. Eight years before that another brief account was printed. This was written by Colonel John S. Ford, a veteran of the Texas Revolution. The colonel had some good material to offer, but sixty years is a long time to hold a sequence of events in the mind, and he filled in with whatever he could get his hands on.

Not published until 1936, although written in 1860, was the pamphlet of Dr. John Sutherland, who left the fort under orders just as the Mexicans were closing in, and so barely missed being in the Alamo during the siege. Nevertheless, he was the only one intimately connected with the fortress who attempted to leave a complete story of what happened. His qualifications for adequacy included interviews with Mrs. Dickenson, Seguin and Smith. Moreover, he was able to question Mexican officers just after they were captured at San Jacinto. In view of these facts, his narrative is at once of great authority and highly disappointing. In the quarter of a century that intervened between the event and his writing many facts had understandably become blurred. Also he glanced at important points and played up minutiae.

Aside from sentimental essays, modern efforts to tell the story have been limited to a chapter by Marquis James, written with his usual well-informed raciness, and an interesting pamphlet by Frederick C. Chabot. Formal scholarship has ignored the story except for Miss Amelia Williams' thoroughgoing analysis, "A Critical Study of the Siege of the Alamo," which is entitled to better distribution than that afforded by the back issues of a periodical.

Many other writers, of course, have enlarged on aspects or dealt with points or persons relative to the Alamo's history. Their consulted works will be found listed in the bibliography which concludes this volume.

J. M. M.

PART I

THE ALAMO AND THE TEXIANS

I

THE MISSION AT BEXAR

THOSE who doubt the greatness of men can leave this book alone or read and recant. This that follows is the story of the siege of the Alamo. It is one of the mightiest tales that the history of this or any nation has to offer. It includes as much of folly in the beginning as it does of magnificence at the end, and is all the better for it. Above all it is, in all its ramifications, the master tale of the American frontier.

Stories from history do not boil into a climax overnight. It took a century and a half to prepare a minor religious structure for winning international fame as a fortress. Reading backward from 1836, the logic of events could be traced to the daydreams of Columbus. Reading forward, the way to the tale can first be followed with the failure of Spanish missions in the Mexican province of Texas. A race along the course from that point in is necessary to an understanding of why the siege took place.

For missions the word "colonization" could be substituted, for the two were interlocked. Along with the mission went the garrison to see that the natives gave a minimum of trouble while undergoing the rigors of conversion. When the tribes had been sufficiently softened by these two agencies, a town would be started and a new region opened to Spanish trade.

If practicality was thus mixed with idealism, it was still the only system of colonizing America which made a place for the Indian in the new world being built. Following the brutal excesses of the conquistadors the rulers of New Spain soberly faced the fact that there would never be enough Spanish immigrants to people the vast region their country claimed. The simplest way to supplement was to incorporate the native population, and this was decided upon. Before the latter could be assimilated, however, it had to learn to submit to the European disciplines of law, labor and religion. The important work of creating new citizens was entrusted, after some experimentation, to missionary specialists with subordinates provided by the regular army.

How well the system worked can be seen from the census taker's findings south of the Rio Grande today. Great nations were colonized by this method, and in all of them the backbone of the population is now native Indian blood. North of the Rio Grande the system was well on the way to proving itself in New Mexico, Arizona and California when annexation by the United States intervened. It never worked satisfactorily in Texas for reasons it is interesting to examine.

To plunge in, no interest in exploiting Texas was shown by the Spaniards until word was passed that La Salle had put the French flag on the Gulf coast. The expedition sent to re-establish Spain's claim included a pair of Franciscan missionaries, primed for business.

These friars, upon whom statesmen banked so heavily, were notable men operating from a mixture of motives. Primarily, there can be no doubt, they were passionate to save the savages from infidelity. At the same time they were patriots, aware of the key part they played in the schemes of the government. They could hardly fail to be, in as much as they were subsidized by the *Audienca* and were under the supervision of the Viceroy of New Spain.

Aside from zeal for the several causes involved, they had to have courage, stamina and a mastery of remarkable techniques. Two or three of them supported by only a few soldiers would go among warrior tribes in the confident expectation that they could not only win them to Christianity but persuade them to settle permanently, doing squaw's work in the shadow of a church. It was this peculiar feature of the Spanish missions—the congregating of Indians into industrious villages—that made the work of the friars at once so difficult and so valuable to the government.

The term the missionaries themselves used for this process was, significantly enough, "reducing." The savages were reduced from proud infidels to humble followers of the Cross. Their tribal structure was destroyed, reducing them from an independent people to the status of minors in a small, provincial Spanish community. From warriors they were reduced to a docile yeomanry that went on the warpath only when drafted for the good of New Spain.

So expert at their work had the friars become that the laws of the Indies allowed them only ten years with a given set of Indians. At the end of that period the missionaries were supposed to leave their converts to the care of the secular church while they pushed on to the next tribe up for reduction.

It was, then, with a confidence justified by experience that the Franciscans planted their first Texas mission in 1693. Even when they were chased back into Mexico a short time later they weren't discouraged. They were used to setbacks and had always won the return engagement. Twenty-three years later they were back again. They would have come before, but the government wouldn't put up the money until France once more made a pass at the province.

This time the preparations for occupation were on a sizable scale. A presidio, guarding a string of three missions, was set up at Nacogdoches in East Texas, where the threat of French infiltration was strongest. To keep watch over the Gulf a presidio-mission combination was established near the mouth of the Lavaca River. Two years later, in 1718, a site on the San Antonio de Padua River was picked to serve as an interior feeder to these outposts.

Leaving the San Antonio colony for later consideration, here's what happened to the above mentioned and subsequent efforts at settlement. The Caddo tribes of northeast Texas were nomads, and well-fed ones at that. They saw no harm in being baptized; but they wouldn't congregate, and that was final. Moreover, they were too numerous and too well supplied with French weapons for the garrison at Nacogdoches to be able to do anything about it.

On the other hand the cannibal Karankawas along the Gulf had consented to congregate and had been rewarded by a lethal epidemic. That was enough for the survivors; they went back to man-eating and successfully resisted all efforts to round them up again. The Mission del Spiritu Sanctu, together with the Labahia Presidio, moved inland once, then again, to the site of Goliad, 150 miles down the San Antonio River from San Antonio itself. There it found some Indians who would listen and functioned after a fashion.

The Nacogdoches missions were also soon in for a rocky time. Seven marauding Frenchmen started rumors of an invading army that sent the garrison sprinting west, a jump ahead of the missions it was supposed to protect. The missions were re-established, but when an inspector found that the three between them didn't have enough settled converts for a game of solitaire they were ordered to set up shop near the Presidio of San Antonio de Bexar. Three later missionary foundations in the Nacogdoches vicinity lasted until 1773 but accomplished nothing.

Other mission efforts can be briefly handled. The one placed among the Tonkawas was a failure. San Saba Missions, which the Apaches euchered the Spanish into founding, was sacked by those redskins, who also murdered the padres. Missions Rosario and Refugio in lower Texas sometimes had converts but more often not.

Presidios were sometimes maintained after missions had been pulled in; but garrisons, though they may earnestly strive to help populate it, do not settle a country. There was, indeed, only one colony in Texas where the classic Spanish pattern of mission, presidio and villa was ever realized. That was the community known by the regional name of Bexar, honoring the Duke of Bexar, later Ferdinand VI.

The presidio, the river on which it was established, and the oldest of the five missions it eventually guarded were all named after St. Anthony. Yet the mission had originally neither been so named or so located. Dedicated by turns to Saints Francis and Joseph, it had occupied three sites south of the Rio Grande before it was decided that it would be of more use in Texas. In 1718 it was ordered to Bexar, where it was soon rechristened San Antonio de Valero. The "Valero" was appended because a nobleman of that name had just become Viceroy of New Spain. Unrecognizable then either by name, appearance or specific location, this was the Alamo.

When the mission was moved, the Indians already congregated, being considered part and parcel of it, had moved north, too. In contact with an unconverted tribe they were valuable as stalking horses, and the Franciscans so used them. In this instance they were particularly useful, for they were Coahuiltecans, a distinction they shared with the numerous little tribes up for reduction.

Calling a powwow, the friars started the process with their usual gambit, salting their promises of spiritual benefits with a demonstration of material ones. Gifts were distributed. Mission Indians told their unbaptized cousins how they dressed fancily, kept warm and ate well all the year around. From time to time the impressive rituals of the Roman church were performed, and the value of baptism in this world as a key to salvation in the next was described.

The rituals no doubt looked like big medicine. Taking care of the belly in this life and the soul in a post-mortem existence are alike pleasant to contemplate. The gifts were rich and novel, and the soldiers promised protection against stronger Indian tribes. It appeared a fine deal from every angle.

Meanwhile the soldiers, busy founding the Presidio of San Antonio de Bexar, had a more complete idea of what they were there for. They would fight pagan tribes if necessary, but their primary duty was to overawe mission Indians during and after conversion. If the Coahuiltecans should yield to persuasion and bribery, so much the better. Otherwise the soldiers were there to see that they crowded together and held still while the twin blessings of salvation and civilization were administered.

To begin with, as it turned out, no force was necessary. The Coahuiltecans fondled their gifts and, never having heard of paternalism, gave it not a thought. They liked the looks of what was being offered and flocked to the Cross in satisfying numbers. Alone of Texas missions, this one got off to a good start.

This promised well for Christendom and Spain. The flaw was that the Coahuiltecans, the only ones who heeded the invitation to the better life, happened to be the weakest and most worthless of all the Texas Indians. Fray Morfi, the Franciscan historian who visited Texas, described the mission Indians as "treacherous," "vile," "lazy," "stupid," and "cowardly." On the other hand he had some rather kind things to say about the Comanches, who gave the friars nothing but the back of the hand.

Right there one of the chief troubles that confronted the whole colonization effort becomes recognizable. Wherever the Spaniards had gained success, they had started in by reducing powerful Indian nations. In Texas they failed utterly to dominate a tribe of any importance. Among the Caddos, the Tonkawas, the Karankawas and the Apaches, they met with every response from polite indifference to bloody assault. The greatest tribe of all, the Comanches, never even gave them a chance to plant a mission.

Elsewhere, however, Spain hadn't let the natives make their own decision. They had usually been able to make it as tough as necessary for any not able to see things their way; and they didn't boggle at partial extermination. Yet in Texas force was as great a failure as religion.

The garrisons of the province weren't large, but they appeared to be large enough. At all times they mustered as many men as Pizarro used to crush the empire of the Incas. Often they had more men than Cortes took against the fierce and populous Aztec nation. As they couldn't make progressive headway in Texas, it must be concluded either that the Indians there were hardier than those previously encountered or that the Spanish soldiers of the day were not such men as had followed the conquistadors. Both were probably the case, and there were additional factors.

To begin with, one of the chief margins of Spanish arms, the cannon, couldn't play its usual overwhelming role. Cannon could play the devil with the towns of the Aztecs, the Incas and the Pueblo Indians, but they weren't so effective against warriors who had no specific points to hold. There was no such thing as besieging and cutting off the supplies of these people. If things looked bad, they skipped away with a mobility Spain herself had supplied. Earlier Indians had found horses awe inspiring as well as terrible in battle. These were expert horsemen. They also knew how to use the muskets the French were careful to furnish.

The Spanish held their own; they were always capable Indian fighters. They scored many victories but never one so decisive that it cleared the savages permanently out of any territory. In particular the Apaches and Comanches continued to take scalps and cattle belonging to citizens of even the relatively successful community of Bexar.

As one of the elements of that community, the garrison should be examined at a little more length. When the friars in charge of founding the colony had planned the Presidio of San Antonio de Bexar they had made specific and unusual requests. They wanted the garrison to be composed of pure-blooded Spaniards, they wanted them all to be of irreproachable character, they wanted them all to be married, and they wanted them all to bring the families to the new country. They did not at all, they emphasized, want any lobos, coyotes or mestizos.

Armies cannot always supply men to serve as models to missionary converts. The army of New Spain could no longer supply men they could certify as Spaniards. The

Franciscans complained that all the men weren't married and that half of those who were had taken the trip to Texas as an occasion for leaving their dependents. There were, the padres pointed out, lobos and coyotes not a few, and a strong percentage of mestizos.

This detachment of outlaws, no-accounts and half-breeds acted about as might be expected. Besides failing to meet the exacting standards of the missionaries, they failed to build a fort worth mentioning. The presidio at Bexar never seems to have been more than an encampment surrounded by a washed-out adobe wall, which in time vanished entirely. The missions all had stone-wall defenses in the course of the years, but the missions had Indian labor. The record is blurred at this point, but apparently the commanders couldn't get the troops to do such heavy work, and the hard-headed padres wouldn't lend their Indians.

Withal it is incredible that a succession of commanders failed to build a stronghold which the constantly marauding Indians would come to fear. The fact that they did not is the turning point in the history of the Alamo.

An informal settlement grew up around the presidio, but it wasn't until 1731 that the Franciscans took the final step in colonization. Encouraged by their success with the Co-ahuiltecans, they asked that a town be founded. As persuasion had brought few immigrants to the new province, the government imported fifteen families from the Canary Islands and shanghaied ten more from the northern part of Mexico proper. When these had arrived, the Villa of San Fernando de Bexar was formally laid out.

With such a nucleus of Spanish citizens, flourishing cities had been built elsewhere in the New World; but the friars just couldn't have any luck in Texas. The Canary Islanders, though peasants and laborers in Europe, immediately adopted a we-came-over-on-the-*Mayflower* attitude. Observing that there was nobody above them, they declared themselves the aristocrats of the land, clamored for Indian servants and complained to the Viceroy when the Franciscans refused to farm the converts out. They had no intention of doing much work themselves and soon found a way to avoid it. In place of showing the converts how civilized people conduct themselves, they went native, living by hunting, fishing and stealing from the missions.

Other settlers came in time, but unsettled conditions enfeebled the attraction. Then trade was effectually banned by Mexico's refusal to permit trade between Texas and its logical market, Louisiana. And a still greater deterrent to immigration was the absence of Indian labor. The ten years allotted the missionaries passed several times over, and still the Indians were not released for exploitation by Mexican pioneers. The friars themselves were infuriated at the delay but refused to let go until they could consider their work well done.

The fact that they could never arrive at such a satisfactory conclusion they blamed upon the Coahuiltecans. The point of view of the Indians didn't come down in the record, so it must be examined from without.

They discovered that along with the spiritual ecstasy of belief went a chilling moral code. They discovered that to obtain the benefits of civilization they must work, men as well as women, and that this sort of thing kept up all the year around. Finally, they discovered that if they objected to anything they found unpleasant they were punished and made to do it into the bargain.

They ran away by ones and by droves—and the padres led the soldiers after them. The friars put their faith in the second generation; but to their astonishment the

Coahuiltecans never developed into dependable citizens. They had a curious habit of backsliding during the summer months and returning to do penance when food became scarce. Sometimes they'd be gone, if they weren't run down in the meantime, for several years. When they finally showed up because they were hungry or because the Apaches were after them, they had forgotten everything they had been taught.

Even those who stayed put didn't give their preceptors much pleasure. They never acquired the faculty of working without direct supervision. Beyond a certain limited point they would develop a passive resistance to self-improvement. They weren't even any good as military auxiliaries who might have helped to keep the blanket Indians at bay. The Franciscans themselves were bold men of action and experienced all the aggravation which negative people arouse in the aggressive. They ended up, as their reports plainly indicate, hating the guts of their spiritual children.

Being the men they were, they held grimly on. They might have made headway if their converts had thriven and multiplied, but when the Coahuiltecans could think of no other way of exasperating the friars, they prematurely turned up their toes and died.

A healthy diet instead of the roots and vermin on which they had formerly often subsisted, food all the year around instead of alternate feast and famine, clean well-made adobe houses instead of wretched little hutches—all these things could reasonably be expected to increase the span of life. They did not.

The five missions in the Bexar community reached a peak of eight or nine hundred among them. Then instead of building up from such a start, the population steadily declined. The death rate enormously exceeded the birth rate, and the deficit had to be supplemented by new converts. There weren't enough Coahuiltecans to keep that up indefinitely. Eventually the supply became exhausted, and there was no other source upon which the missions could draw.

The Franciscans had other troubles, too. No matter how many times the personnel of the presidio changed, the padres on deck weren't satisfied with the co-operation given. They claimed that the soldiers were too cruel to some Indians and much too affectionate toward others. They claimed that the soldiers shirked their job as labor supervisors. They claimed the soldiers connived with the townsmen to steal from the missions. Most bitterly of all, they complained that the soldiers were lackadaisical about running fugitive converts to earth.

No group at Bexar respected any other. The friars complained about the cattle thieving and general worthlessness of the civil population. The settlers did live by thievery, but, letting that pass, they had much to say in reply. They blamed the poverty of the region on the fact that in place of having been congregated the Indians had been sucked down the mission drain, leaving almost none alive to make themselves useful. They pointed out, moreover, that the missions retained possession of the richest lands long after there were enough natives to utilize so much acreage. Repeatedly they asked the government to recall the friars, and finally their request was granted.

It was in 1793 that the Mission of San Antonio de Valero was finally secularized. After seventy-five years it retained only forty-three settled converts; the other four local missions averaged about as many apiece. Except for a modest number of half-breeds, to which they'd contributed their share of genes, this was all that was left of the Coahuiltecans.

There was another small group of converted Indians at Labahia, and that was the lot for Texas. The effort to make the natives the main core of the province's population had come to nothing.

Yet Mission Valero, as the Franciscans short-named it, did exist for three quarters of a century, and during that time hundreds of men and women worked on it. Something was built; in point of fact, it was built several times.

The original adobe and thatch chapel stood on the west bank of the San Antonio River, on the same side as the presidio. In a year or so it was moved; then, possibly to get the female converts away from the lobos, coyotes and mestizos, it was shifted across the stream. It wasn't until 1744 that the usual stone mission was erected.

Witness any number of examples, the Franciscans habitually built for the ages. The chapel in question lasted several years and inexplicably collapsed. It wasn't until 1757 that the structure shown in all the Texas travel booklets was begun. It was handsomely designed in the classic mission manner, with simple, massive lines, softened by decoration only on the façade. For some reason the bell tower—or twin towers, as certain authorities believe—which the plans called for, was never added, and the interior remained unfinished. Then, curiously enough, there was a second disaster springing from faulty construction. The roof caved in, though there is some question as to whether this happened before or soon after the mission was secularized.

In the days of their functioning there was, of course, much more to missions than the chapels, which is about all that remains to be seen of any of them now. In its complete form the establishment was a combination monastery, guest hostel, jail, school, factory and walled town as well as church. Mission Valero had all these features. In an inner court

stood the quarters of the padres, a two-story building connected with the chapel by a cloister. Here also were the
looms where the Indian women made homespun fabrics.
Here were quarters for the soldiers detailed to ride herd
on the converts, as well as a roomy jail for Indians who
backslid.

Beyond the inner court was a plaza with a wall around
it. In this enclosure, sealed with a gate guarded by three
cannon, were the adobe houses of the natives. By day they
worked in the extensive, irrigated fields or looked after the
large herds of cattle and horses. By night the wall protected them from the Apaches, the evil example of soldiers
and other laymen, not to mention their own low impulses.
To prevent skulduggery within this sanctuary, unwed men
and women were locked up at curfew.

For lack of Indians to keep it in repair, the wall had
partially crumbled before the establishment was secularized.
Years ago, however, Valero and the other missions had
ceased to be the most important feature of the Bexar settlement. With the missions declining, the bulk of the population slowly became concentrated in the civil community. The
place, indeed, came to be thought of not as a cluster of missions, a garrison and a town, but as a town only, of which
the other institutions were mere appendages.

San Fernando de Bexar was not only the capital but the
gem of Spanish Texas. And it was, we have Fray Morfi's
word for it, no more than a collection of wretched shanties,
brightened by only a handful of better-looking buildings.
A typical census of the late eighteenth century shows that the
population totaled seventeen hundred, including garrison
troops and mission Indians. Of these, three or four hundred were recognized as Spanish, and in Mexico there was
already a liberal interpretation of that term. The rest, aside

from the Indians, were unquestioned mestizos and culebras. Where the mulattoes came from isn't clear, but they suddenly appear in the census records outnumbering both the half-breeds and the Indians. No doubt there was as much redskin as African in most of them.

In the rest of the huge province, eight hundred to a thousand more were reckoned subjects of Spain. In addition to a garrison or so these could be found at Labahia, where a small civil community had grown up around the mission, and at a scratch settlement at Nacogdoches whose history is not pertinent here. That was all. The government of New Spain had spent millions of pesos. The Franciscans had lost their lives in martyrdom or worn them away in successive generations of service. There had been elaborate military expeditions. Loyal civil servants had given their years to the project. Nothing brought satisfactory results. Nothing worked as it did in other countries into which Spain had put its strength.

The government finally became so disgusted that it decided against further efforts at colonization until the settling of European wars should release more money and enough troops for a full-scale conquest of the entire region. For all the money that had been spent on Texas there had been hardly a peso of revenue in return. Meanwhile, the incessant wars with Apaches and Comanches came high, and the soldiers in solitary outposts were keeping a fruitless vigil.

It was almost decided to retire to the Rio Grande, but the official charged with reorganizing the border defenses hesitated to abandon San Fernando. In the end, it was made one of the three outposts of the northern frontier. The other two were Santa Fe, New Mexico, and Natchitoches, which Spain had acquired when France ceded Louisiana in 1762. The remaining garrisons in Texas were pulled south.

Spanish Texas, early in the nineteenth century. The point ma

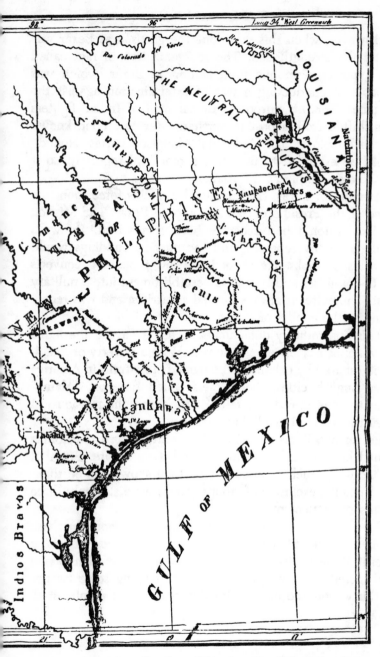

St. Louis is where La Salle planted his short-lived French colony.

However, when this was done the garrison at Bexar was materially strengthened. The reorganization in fact called for a powerful mobile unit, station at Bexar, which was capable of conducting a war of extermination against the Apaches. For this purpose a detachment of Indian fighters was shifted from a post in northern Mexico proper, known as the Pueblo of San Carlos del Alamo de Parras. Nobody could be expected to use such a mouthful regularly, so it was known simply as the Alamo.

Arriving in Texas, the commander of this force found no trace of the Presidio of San Antonio de Bexar. The Mission of San Antonio had recently been secularized. Its walls could be easily repaired, and the mission buildings would serve as barracks. He shooed the few remaining converts off the premises and turned the establishment into a military post. Thereafter it always housed a garrison and was recognized as the citadel of Bexar.

This first military detachment to use it gave it the name by which it has since been known. With a poverty of imagination shared by colonists who named cross-trails in America after English cities, the soldiers called the post "Alamo" after the one they'd just left. It stuck, and the mission lost even the name of a religious structure.

Perversely, Texas did a little better after efforts to colonize it had been abandoned than it had done before. But that isn't saying much. The census of 1800 showed three thousand people, exclusive of troops. There were still only three points of settlement.

That was the situation when the Louisiana Purchase brought United States pioneers to the Texas border. Looking over it, these insatiable land-grabbers saw a marvelously rich and incredibly huge province which, barring some twenty or thirty thousand blanket Indians, was all but uninhabited.

II

FILIBUSTERS AND SETTLERS

EVEN before the Louisiana Purchase, amateur American conquistadors had their eyes on the emptiness of Texas. National attention was also drawn to the province by colonial Spanish policy.

Although Louisiana permitted United States immigration and trade, Mexico banned both these forms of international intercourse. In consequence, smuggling not only flourished but was genteel.

As early as 1785, a man named Philip Nolan had been engaged in rounding up Texas horses for sale east of the Mississippi. Through a lapse of memory Edward Everett Hale gave his full name to *The Man Without a Country,* who was really supposed to be a younger brother of the adventurer. The actual Philip Nolan is said to have been a man whose unusual attainments recommended him to the attention of Thomas Jefferson. An even more interesting fact about him is that he was a protégé of General James Wilkinson.

The latter dealt from the bottom of the deck more consistently than anybody in American history who was permitted to die peaceably and at large. Before qualifying to become a figure in this chronicle, he had conspired against George Washington, George Rogers Clark and Mad Anthony Wayne. He had also contracted to sell Kentucky to Spain. In the course of this deal he secretly became a Spanish citizen. He neither renounced that citizenship nor ceased to draw Spanish pay as an under-cover operative when he became Commander of the Army of the United States at the close of the eighteenth century.

Just how far his designs against Mexico had progressed at this time can't be ascertained; but his man Nolan entered Texas with a well-armed body of volunteers in 1800. Ostensibly this was another mustang raid, but it was actually a reconnaissance in force. What happened to the expedition wasn't known in America until a man called Peter Ellis Bean published a dramatic narrative following his escape from prison some years later. The party had outbluffed one Spanish patrol but didn't do so well with the larger one that eventually cornered it. In the ensuing battle Nolan was killed and the survivors of the detachment were captured.

Before Wilkinson could find another cat's paw, a bigger thief intervened. Violating a sworn agreement, Napoleon double-crossed Spain by selling Louisiana to the United States.

There had already been threats of war because the Governor of Louisiana had taken it upon himself to close the Mississippi to United States shipping. The Purchase made more trouble. At first Spain wasn't going to get out of Louisiana, but when she finally consented to do that she was outraged to find that Jefferson expected her to get out of Texas, too. To make his sale more attractive Napoleon had revived old French claims and thrown them into the kitty.

Jefferson certainly believed that the United States had bought everything east of the Rio Grande, including not only Texas but half of New Mexico. Spain wasn't moved by Napoleon's generosity. She pointed out that the province had always been administered as a part of Mexico, not of Louisiana. She also strengthened her hold on Texas.

It's a truism that governments seldom operate efficiently until they're squeezed by violence or the threat of it. Within a year Spain put more colonists north of the Rio Grande than she'd been able to do in any two decades of the preceding century. New settlements were started, and the garrisons were strengthened, particularly along the eastern border.

As it happened, Spain and France had never got around to settling just where Texas left off and Louisiana began; and after Spain was possessed of both it didn't much matter. She had no survey to fall back on, but she did have the historic fact that the eastern outpost of Texas had formerly been the Presidio of Los Adaes. The long-abandoned fort had been located seven miles west of the Red River, about on a level with Natchitoches, Louisiana. Determining to reoccupy the site, Spain threw troops across the Sabine.

American officials had meanwhile decided that at least part of the western boundary of Louisiana was what it is today, that same Sabine River. Whether Texas still belonged to Spain or not, this eastward thrust represented territorial invasion in American eyes, as the local commander of United States forces pointed out. The Spaniards consented to withdraw, pending arbitration, but not an inch farther than the Sabine. At this crisis Wilkinson arrived.

Throughout the boundary dispute, which lasted many months, the general had been very busy. Ignoring the awkward diplomatic situation, he had sent Lieutenant Zebulon

Pike on an unauthorized mission into New Mexico. He had enlisted British interest in an invasion of Spanish holdings. He had earned his pay from Spain by warning her United States ambassador that England was up to no good. And he had entrapped the imagination of America's arch-ogre, Aaron Burr.

With Wilkinson, the plan to steal Texas or New Mexico or to conquer Mexico itself—all three schemes have been attributed to him at one time or another—may never have been anything more than a scheme for extortion. As it is not shown that he made any overt moves himself, it is possible that from the days of Philip Nolan on he was inciting filibusters in order that Spain might continue to find him a useful informer. Whatever else he was, and he was very many things, Aaron Burr was no such fourflusher. He took the nebulous plan which Wilkinson confided to him and, in his own words, "matured it."

Energetically traveling around the country, he began gathering an expeditionary force as well as the shipping necessary to carry it down the Mississippi. It was understood by Burr that Wilkinson would desert his post upon signal and join him in the venture.

In the meantime, the General had got into one of his periodic difficulties with the government. Adroit as he was at keeping down wind, the smell of his activities betimes reached the capital and moved politicians to ask for his head. There was also danger that Spain had at length discovered that a traitor can't be trusted and would take revenge by telling of his long duplicity. A lesser scoundrel might have ducked for cover. Wilkinson came out of his corner like a Hollywood cowboy, shooting in all directions at once and scoring with every shot.

To Jefferson he reported first that he was on the trail of

a great conspiracy, then that he had succeeded in identifying the guilty party. According to him, and the accusation that ruined Burr had no other support, Burr was not only planning to invade Mexico but to detach Kentucky, Tennessee and the whole Louisiana Purchase from the Union. Wilkinson asked compensation for the large sums he had personally spent while unearthing this plot. P.S. He cashed in.

To Spain, the General reported the same thing, less the parts that would be of no interest to that country. For this proof of loyalty he asked for a reward, which was duly forwarded. Next in his capacity of Commander of the United States Army he rushed to the point where American and Spanish troops were barking at each other across the Sabine. Conferring with the Spanish commander, he made a treaty calling for a stretch of neutral ground as a buffer between the two countries.

He had absolutely no authority to make a treaty and neither had the Spanish officer. Considering that the United States claimed Texas and more, whereas the designated Neutral Ground was all east of the Sabine, the terms were most unfavorable to America. But Wilkinson's luck held. The administration didn't want war and was grateful for a treaty which allowed postponement of a definite stand. Less surprisingly, Spain gave the terms and the General her blessing, and the treaty went through. Wilkinson was complimented all around.

Things were looking better, but the General hadn't quite finished. To prevent Burr from telling whose idea it was in the first place, he had his partner arrested and preferred charges of treason. As the star witness for the prosecution he perforce then journeyed east, but he left a troublesome legacy in the form of the Neutral Ground.

Into this area over which neither Spain nor the United

States had jurisdiction there promptly went men who had no use for jurisdiction anyhow. Reputedly one of the most savage groups of bandits who have ever terrorized any part of North America, they preyed without discrimination upon settlers on both sides of their domain as well as upon the smugglers plying between them.

For Mexico, at least, this was a minor affliction. The priest, Hidalgo had launched a revolt against Spanish rule, and by 1810 civil war had reached Texas. The garrison of the Alamo declared for liberty and a hypothetical republic; but the leader became the first commander of that fortress who was martyred for freedom. The rebellion, however, was not crushed by executing leaders, even Hidalgo himself. It was destined to be the major activity of the country for more than a decade.

Having no such distraction, the United States took operations in the Neutral Ground much more seriously. Eventually a punitive force commanded by a Lieutenant Augustus Magee was charged with breaking up the bandit gangs. The young officer did his job efficiently; but in addition to killing, capturing and flogging bandits he looked across the Sabine into Texas.

Magee wasn't being promoted, it seemed to him, as fast as he deserved to be. In Texas, he had been informed, the cause of liberty was being lost for lack of a commander. Resigning his lieutenancy, he elected himself colonel and started collecting followers.

He began by enlisting the bandits who had survived his law enforcement methods. Having observed that it was safer to be on his side than against him, they joined up in some numbers; yet, it was more than a band of desperadoes who entered Texas in 1812. If the shelving of the border dispute had satisfied the government, it had never satisfied the citizenry of the United States. Almost every American believed that Texas rightfully belonged to the Union. It followed that aggression against Spain, the nation withholding the province, was an act of piety.

Magee was shrewd enough to see, however, that he couldn't expect to attract Mexican support, even for liberty, in the name of an American invader. To draw local adherents he produced a fugitive republican called Bernado Guttierez and made him nominal commander. It was this mixed force, including some bands of Indians, that invoked the existence of the first State of Texas.

The expedition defeated the Spanish garrison at Nacogdoches and scored a couple of other victories before being halted by a force operating out of Labahia. Here under disputed circumstances Colonel Magee died, and the command of American Volunteers passed to Colonel Samuel Kemper.

In a pitched battle Kemper crushed the Spanish royalists at Labahia and went on to score a much more important victory over the Alamo garrison at Bexar. This had the look of success. All Spanish forces in Texas had been conquered. The repeated triumphs had inspired many Mexicans with zeal for liberty. American opportunists, including the son of General James Wilkinson, were flocking to a good thing as fast as their horses would bring them. Even if Mexico couldn't be overrun it looked as though Texas could be held.

At this juncture the Mexican officers with the rebel forces decided to settle a grudge. Kemper had given the Governor of Texas and the royalist officers generous terms when they surrendered. That wasn't the way the Mexican revolution was being fought, however. Guttierez or some of his associates had the prisoners marched a few miles from Bexar and cut their throats. This was the first massacre of a garrison of the Alamo, and it is noteworthy that it was not wrought by the forces of oppression but by the sponsors of freedom.

The American Volunteers, such of them as weren't cut-throats themselves, were disgusted; and the unity of the force was destroyed. Many Americans left for home. Kemper either washed his hands of Mexican independence or returned to enlist more volunteers, depending on the authority followed, and he either did or did not return for the ensuing battles. In any case, the command of the Americans passed to Colonel Henry Perry. Guttierez had been deposed following the massacre of the prisoners, and a dubious character named Jose Alvarez de Toledo took his place.

Against the vanguard of the royalist army sent to recapture Bexar, the republicans scored one last victory. When the main body drew near, however, they couldn't get together on just what to do. Toledo didn't want to be just a figurehead, and the Americans refused to follow his orders. It was a bad time for this to happen, for the leader of the approaching troops was General Joaquin de Arredondo, an experienced and wily field commander.

By ordering a retreat he sucked the Americans—most of the Mexicans and Indians had refused to fight—into a position where he had them in enfilade from two sides. At that, frontier marksmanship came within an ace of getting the upper hand, but that wasn't good enough. In the upshot, the Volunteers were broken, and the long death roll included the State of Texas.

Some of the fugitives were hunted down and killed on the spot, some were caught and formally executed, some were caught and ultimately deported. Among those lucky enough to escape entirely was Perry; but he couldn't stand prosperity. A few years later, in 1816, he was associated with a

Spanish liberal and an aide of Bolivar's on Galveston Island. The scheme that time was to attack Mexico by sea as well as by land; but the operation was a failure, and Perry didn't survive his second try.

The most noteworthy result of his sojourn on the island was that it attracted Jean Lafitte's attention to the advantages of Galveston. The place offered the likeliest combination of hide-out and good anchorage that he'd found since he'd left Barataria to oblige the United States Navy. Therefore when Perry et al launched their attack on the mainland he and his pirates moved in behind them. Lafitte also elected himself a defender of Mexican independence. He called himself Governor of Galveston and had as much right to the title as a group of exiled republicans could bestow. With this warrant he preyed on Spanish shipping, and so successfully that Spain ceased to be the dominant maritime power in the Gulf. He also founded a town whose citizens were exclusively buccaneers, whores, fences and fugitive criminals. He called it Campeachy and ruled it from La Maison Rouge, the luxurious brick mansion he'd furnished with loot.

The pirates held their grip on Texas soil far longer than any other Americans who came to the province to make their fortune by force of arms. For that reason they were the last of this class of immigrant, but before the United States Navy again sent them on their way—Lafitte wasn't always able to tell a Spanish ship from an American one—there was one more all-out attempt to detach Texas from Mexico.

James Long, who appointed himself general on the strength of having served as a medical officer at the Battle of New Orleans, was the organizer of this effort. It is perhaps only a coincidence that he had married a niece of General James Wilkinson, and it is claimed for him that he was a high-minded man. At the least it should be said in his favor that he didn't mask his intentions by a feigned zeal for Mexican liberation. Believing, as nearly all Americans did, that Texas was rightfully United States territory, he plainly stated that it was his ambition to restore the region to his country. Gathering the usual collection of young adventurers, republican zealots, ruffians and patriots, he established a foothold in 1819 and tried to rally the sparse citizenry to him.

As the native sons showed no disposition to help separate Texas from the rest of Mexico, General Long turned elsewhere for assistance. Pirate or not, Lafitte still ranked as the man who was pardoned by the President of the United States for fidelity at the Battle of New Orleans, where Long had presumably met him. Moreover, he was the sworn foe of the Spaniards. The general sent a letter to Campeachy, suggesting joint operations, and eventually went there to hold council.

The remarkable truth is that although Lafitte was smashing Spanish commerce, he was nevertheless a paid spy of Spanish officialdom. The latter seem to have taken the practical viewpoint that he was going to raid their shipping anyhow and that they might as well make what use of him they could. In this instance he earned his money by betraying Long's plans to the royalists, who snapped up the General's scattered posts and nearly nabbed the General himself. Jean Lafitte, as Byron pointed out in *The Corsair*, had had his one moment of virtue and was content to rest on his laurels.

Long tried again almost immediately but with no better success and worse personal luck. This time the royalists collared him, and he spent the following months working his way south, jail by jail. Yet when he reached Mexico City, where he was finally sent for trial, and undoubtedly execution, he found that he was no enemy of the government after all. For by then it was 1821 and the forces of rebellion had at last put down Spanish rule. A man thus reprieved might be expected to be careful of his life, but Long succeeded in getting himself shot before he could leave the Mexican capital.

As far as the prosperity of Texas was concerned, the sum of all these attempts to seize, save or annex it was evil. The Spanish method of crushing revolts called for destroying the life and property of anybody who couldn't prove he had never thought of rebelling. Arredondo alone eradicated most of the population gains that the province had made since the turn of the century. At the date of Mexican secession Texas had only three thousand civilians and had been reduced to only two points of settlement. Nacogdoches had been wiped out, leaving only Labahia and San Fernando de Bexar.

The latter was still the largest town. A few substantial merchants lived there, but in all Texas there was almost no profitable development. The way of life of the inhabitants owed much more than ever to the Indians, for agriculture had declined since the day of the missions.

The problem of the Indians themselves had grown more serious instead of simpler. The Comanches had driven the Apaches away—something the Spaniards had never succeeded in doing—and Bexar was their oyster. Whenever they felt like it they took over the town, making, it is charged, the garrison look after their horses. Moreover the savage population of the province had increased as the tribes pushed west to get clear of the United States or were moved bodily in conformance with American policy. The Caddos, for instance, had become a plains tribe of central Texas instead of a forest tribe ranging the eastern marches. The

Cherokees, formerly of North Carolina and Tennessee, were beginning to dominate northeastern Texas.

Meanwhile relations with the United States had temporarily improved. In 1819 Spain had ceded Florida in exchange, among other things, for the surrender of claims to Texas. A treaty of amity was thrown in which at last permitted peaceful immigration into the province.

There were strings. Everyone entering to settle had to become a Spanish subject and, by that token, a Catholic. Some may have been deterred, but that wasn't the type of thing to give the average pioneer much concern. In chief, they recognized the responsibility of looking after their families in a savage world. Weighed against that, religion and citizenship in their own country rode high. Texas looked good to them.

Yet it must not be understood that indiscriminate settlement on the part of foreigners was tolerated. The Mexican authorities knew too much about American frontiersmen to want to leave them to their own unfettered devices. The system evolved was to lease grants to individuals known as *empresarios*. The latter were responsible for introducing an allotted number of families and for seeing that the land was properly distributed. They were also held responsible for the good character of the colonists they brought in. The penalty for bad judgment or maladministration was forfeiture of grant.

The reason for Spain's change of heart about immigration was the hope that American colonies would serve as a buffer between Mexican settlements and the Indians. It had got to the point where there was no safe communication between Bexar and Labahia even. The road from San Fernando to Santa Fe couldn't be negotiated by less than a company of soldiers. The way south to Mexico proper was almost as dangerous. Something had to be done, and the Spanish themselves hadn't been able to do it. Also, the government hoped for an industrious class of farmers such as its own colonization efforts had failed to produce.

So in her own deliberate fashion Spain acted. That is to say that although immigration was legal in 1819, the dicker with the first *empresario* wasn't concluded until 1821. There were many candidates, including the aged General James Wilkinson, but the one in question was Moses Austin, who died of the hardships incurred in putting the deal through. It looked as if Stephen his son had inherited a good thing; but just as he had settled the final details with the government, he learned that it had no power to act. As stated above, Mexico's long effort to break away from Spain had finally succeeded.

Stephen Austin went to Mexico City prepared to press his claims on the new republic, only to find that it was an empire instead. It took him nearly a year to butter the Emperor sufficiently to gain his backing, but Agustin I at length agreed to help him. Unfortunately for both Austin and Agustin I, the latter had to leave his empire about that time, for it was turning into a democracy after all. Austin had his work to do all over again with the newly created congress; but in 1824 he was at last authorized to start his colony.

This was only one of the things significant to the history of the Alamo which took place in 1824. The Constitution of the United States of Mexico did not recognize Texas as a national subdivision entitled, as it always had been in the past, to its own government. Instead it was combined with the old province of Coahuila, just below the Rio Grande in central Mexico, to make the State of Coahuila-Texas. Saltillo in southern Coahuila became the capital, and Bexar was shorn of what little glory it possessed.

The reason given for this readjustment was that Texas didn't have enough of a population to justify separate statehood, which was certainly the case. However, the constitution provided that Texas could regain its status as an entity when, as and if the number of inhabitants warranted it.

The incoming colonists were untroubled by what had happened at the time. For a year or so, in fact, they were untroubled by Mexican officialdom at all. Authority for ruling the various grants was vested in Austin and the *empresarios* who followed him in obtaining concessions. Even the delicate matter of religion wasn't pressed. On the contrary, the colonists complained that priests seldom showed up to perform such basic rites as those of baptism and wedding.

The North Americans, as the Mexicans called them, had a hard time at first, but they were workers and fighters. They made the wilderness produce and taught the Indians caution. The experiment was a success, and the government congratulated itself upon having moved wisely.

At precisely this juncture the ghost of an old evil came back to raise Cain. There had been no bad feeling adjunct to settling any of the grants except the one which took in the old settlement of Nacogdoches. Arredondo's men had chased the survivors from that desolated town, forbidding them to return. But that had been the work of the Royalists; and the Republic, recognizing the victims as martyrs, revalidated the land claims. Well and good, except that it was done after the distribution of land to American settlers had already been started. Furthermore, as the records of Nacogdoches had burned with the town, anybody who could buy witnesses could claim what he wished. Often the Mexicans claimed land which had already been improved by hardworking North American frontiersmen.

Whenever the claims of foreigners impinge on those of the native born there's the makings of trouble. The North Americans felt that they were being cheated with the connivance of the government. The Mexicans declared that interlopers were robbing them of their birthright.

That the Mexican government did in fact prove more sympathetic to those of their own tribe than to the newcomers was only natural; but that didn't soothe Colonel Haden Edwards, the local *empresario,* who was disposed to uphold what he considered his rights with strong measures. The Governor of Coahuila-Texas countered by voiding his grant and ordering him into exile. That might have been all there was to it if the Colonel's brother, Ben Edwards, hadn't been a man of hot blood and imagination.

After excited appeals, containing more high-flown rhetoric than Burke and Paine could muster between them, he raised the red and white banner of Fredonia to the startled view of the few near enough to behold it. He likewise published a declaration of independence which let the world know that Fredonians weren't to be trifled with while a just God reigned in Heaven.

Examined, Fredonia turned out to be nothing less than the old province of Texas, remarkably divided. To the north of a given line the land would be held by twenty-three Indian tribes, which Edwards claimed for allies. South of it the North Americans and all right-minded Mexicans would hold forth. After the necessary war to establish their independence, all Fredonians would return to their respective wigwams and ploughs to dwell forever after in an amity untroubled by infringement on each other's territory.

For the backing he believed the Indians would give him Edwards relied on the promises of Cherokee chiefs, of whom the most influential were Big Mush and the Bowl. That the other American colonists would join him Edwards never doubted. In this faith he routed the local Mexican garrison and waited hopefully for friends to rally around.

Mostly he waited in vain. Big Mush, the Bowl and most of their satellite chieftains welched, and the only two who tried to keep their word were murdered by their fellow-tribesmen. The conduct of most of the North Americans was even more disappointing to the founders of the new republic.

One of the duties of an *empresario* was to act as the local commander of militia. Austin promptly fulfilled his obligation by gathering his settlers and marching against Nacogdoches, the Fredonian capital. To make the odds even greater, Colonel Bean, once a follower of Philip Nolan but now an officer of the Mexican army, persuaded many of the Indians actually to side against Fredonia, thus strengthening the force of regulars he led to squelch the revolt. The citizens of the impromptu state were quickly vanquished and soon pardoned; but the comic episode left a bitter train.

The correctness with which Austin and other North Americans had lived up to their oath of loyalty should have convinced the Mexican authorities that they had nothing to fear from the new citizens as a whole. Fredonia, however, had given the government a scare from which it refused to recover.

The Indian population of the territory was at last being matched in numbers. The border was secure as never before. Agriculture was flourishing, and so was trade. Seaports were being developed. The individual enterprise of men willing to do the work themselves had succeeded where the government and self-appointed conquerors had failed; but the authorities didn't like it. They could only think of the damage it was possible for the colonists, so near their aggressive parent country, to accomplish if they should unite in revolt.

The promising settlements were never afterward left to themselves but were subjected to increasingly severe federal control. Furthermore, the medium of enforcement was military power, the source of authority which history has shown that the civilian of Anglo-Celtic extraction most resents.

This notwithstanding, the colonies throve. So did Bexar, where trade naturally prospered with the growth of the state. Prosperity had attracted so many Mexican immigrants that it almost began to deserve the title of city which had been formally bestowed on San Fernando as far back as 1811. It was still commonly known just as Bexar; but around 1824 it began to be officially called San Antonio and is so shown on a Mexican map of 1826. On the other hand a Mexican map of 1835 shows it as San Fernando.

However it was officially styled, it continued to be the metropolis of the territory; but it was nearly all that remained of Spanish Texas. As reconstituted, Nacogdoches was largely an American town, and Labahia—already called Goliad as an anagram in honor of Hidalgo, the first Mexican revolutionist—was in a district also dominated by North Americans. All in all immigrants from the United States outnumbered Mexicans three or four to one in 1830.

III

MEXICO VS. THE TEXIANS

FREDONIA cast its largest shadow several years after its demise. In 1830 the Mexican government, convinced that it had a cuckoo in the nest, took steps to stunt the growth of the North American colonies.

The method adopted must have cost its creators a great deal of thought, for the implementing act is one of the most curious on the books of any nation. Granted, the said creators were in an awkward position. Mexico could not flatly ban United States immigration without risking a severance of diplomatic relations. So the statute specified, in effect, that no person from a nation bordering upon Mexico could settle in a Mexican state contiguous to the country from which he came. As far as Texas was concerned, this was turning off the tap.

The North Americans had reason to protest. They had gone through the bad years when fields had to be chopped out of the woods and when an Indian raid was commoner than a square meal. And now when the country was ripe for development they were denied the prosperity which could only be achieved through the growth of their communities.

This, however, was only their sorest grievance among many. Everything began to be taxed, and import duties were so high that legitimate trade in many important items was out of the question. Then towns were ridden by garrisons whose rank and file conducted themselves as if they were holding down a hostile foreign country. Military rule overrode civil rule whenever a local commander felt like throwing his weight about.

In addition, things which had not seemed so bad at first had rotted into cankers. The Mexican Constitution of 1824 was a liberal document for a people who had never previously enjoyed the slightest degree of home rule. To men who had lived under that of the United States, on the other hand, it was lacking in several major respects. Notably, there was no provision for trial by jury, nor were courts open to public examination.

The enforced alliance with Coahuila was likewise a growing aggravation. The wealth and therefore the interests of that region lay in mining, whereas Texas was given over to agriculture and stock raising. As the Coahuila representatives in the state legislature outnumbered those from Texas ten to two, acts favorable to Coahuila only were the ones chiefly considered and passed.

Then Texas had no superior court of its own. Those called to justice or demanding a settlement of rights had to travel five hundred miles by horseback. The intervening country was not only rough, desiccated and largely deserted, it was also not quite deserted enough. Scalp-hunting Indians made the trip to Saltillo, the state capital, a perilous undertaking.

In 1832 the administration thought up a new and ingenious way to hamstring the colonies. Negro slavery was abolished, a measure that sounds altruistic but was scarcely so in intent. As the missions had failed to reduce local Indians, the decree produced a labor problem in Texas only. The millions of Indians who worked in the mines or manned the vast ranches in other sections of Mexico were not affected by the emancipation act.

The North Americans as well as some Mexican citizens of Texas began to crave separate statehood as the only hope for even a partial improvement in conditions. But there again the anti-immigration act of 1830 interfered. The constitution specified that a population of eighty thousand was requisite, and Texas couldn't muster that many even if counting blanket Indians was allowable. Of course, some Americans still dribbled in—adventurers, and as often as not unwanted ones rather than settlers of the type originally invited—but not enough to approach making up the count.

Nevertheless, this new element, restless and largely free of the sobering influence of family responsibilities, was important. If many were ruffians or even out and out fugitives from the laws of the United States, quite a few were aggressive young professional men, capable of giving voice and direction to the feeling that something toward counteracting injustice ought to be done.

Finally the lid blew off in 1832 at the Port of Anahuac on Galveston Bay. Colonel Juan Bradburn, who commanded the fort there, was the senior officer on the Gulf and had taken advantage of his position to be particularly objectionable in his dealings with the colonists. His men naturally took their cue from their leader. The clash between citizens and soldiers which eventually took place resulted in the imprisoning of certain local residents, infuriating all the rest. The word spread to the other colonies, and overnight most of the North Americans were in revolt against their garrison rulers.

It should be pointed out that Bradburn had some points on his side. The Mexican government had instigated persecution, and the Colonel had taken advantage of the government's attitude to indulge an aptitude for sadism. But, granting all that, the peace was certainly being flouted by the citizenry.

The Texians, as they came to call themselves, were frontiersmen. As a group the records show them to have been singularly law abiding to begin with; but they knew how to make it just as tough as the traffic could bear if that's what it took to get by. Certainly they did things which no government in the world could overlook and still keep any pretense to authority.

Heavy import duties on essential commodities drove them to smuggling, which authorities can wink at if it's done with a show of secrecy. By and by the Texians got tired of being secretive. Once, at least, a known smuggler cleared port by daylight, protected from hovering revenue collectors by the guns of cheering men ashore. An official messenger of the government, bearing information about climbing tariffs, was mobbed in plain sight of the Mexican naval vessel which brought him. One enterprising smuggler bought a couple of cannon in New Orleans to protect his ship against government vessels.

These were the men whom Bradburn had set himself to intimidate. Accepting his seizure of their associates as the point where they must force recognition of their civil rights at all costs, the colonists of the vicinity assembled under arms. While they were marching to present Bradburn with an ultimatum, a detachment of Mexican cavalry stumbled into them and was captured. That looked like the right answer. A simple exchange of prisoners was proposed to the colonel, who agreed. Further bloodshed would have been avoided had he but kept his word, but he took his own men back without surrendering the imprisoned Texians.

The colonists looked the situation over. To batter a way into the fort protecting the garrison would require cannon, and the only ones procurable belonged to the smuggler who had purchased two in New Orleans and who lived sixty crow-flight miles away in Brazoria. John Austin—no kin to Stephen—in command, the rescue party marched to the inland port of Brazoria and took ship. Then, with the cannon aboard, the expedition dropped down the Brazos River, prepared to sail north around into Galveston Bay and so into Anahuac Harbor.

At the mouth of the river the guns of the fort at Velasco made it unwise to proceed without permission, so Austin went ashore. With shameless brass he asked the commander of the fort to let him slip by with the cannon, so that he could use them against the commander's superior officer. When the request was refused it was agreed to attack the fort and silence its batteries.

This was the first engagement of the revolt where casualties were heavy. The cannon on the schooner kept up a long distance duel with the guns of the fort, now perforce divided to face in several directions. The real damage, however, was done by individual marksmen. These hunters, who could kill a squirrel with a heavy caliber rifle without damaging the meat, were not likely to miss a man. When a Mexican exposed a hand in servicing a cannon, he got a hole through it; and the number of defenders reported as so incapacitated was terrific. Many were killed outright in this battle, though not all on one side. Riflemen seldom face shrapnel with impunity.

At length the garrison had so many dead and disabled there weren't enough left to man the walls. Velasco fell, giving the Texians their first major victory. John Austin was prepared to follow it up by smoking Bradburn out of Anahuac, now that he was free to transport his cannon, but circumstances interceded. Colonel Jose de las Piedras, commander of the garrison at Nacogdoches and senior officer in all East Texas, came to investigate the reported trouble and didn't bring enough men with him. The Texians snapped him up and were once more in a position to do business.

After hearing their grievances Piedras promised to put Bradburn under arrest for abusing authority he didn't have. He also promised to release the captive colonists. The Texians took him at his word and this time made no mistake. Piedras was honorable.

The North Americans had scored. It remained to find out what, aside from a few lives and wounds, they had to pay for it. They were armed rebels who had achieved a victory over the military power of their adopted country. And it was a country where the method of punishing revolt was known to reach the extreme of brutality.

Distance—they were fifteen hundred miles by bad roads from Mexico City—and political conditions were alike on their side at the time. Mexico was in a highly involved state of civil war and had been for some years. The principle of becoming president by election was not revered by unelected politicians. Having failed at the hustings, Vicente Guerrero took the presidency from the people's choice, Gomez Pedraza, by an appeal to arms and was inaugurated in 1829. Nine months later he was deposed by his Vice-President, Anastasio Bustamente, who had him scragged into the bargain.

In 1829, too, Spain made its last effort to reconquer Mexico. By repulsing the invaders at Tampico, Santa Anna had become a national hero controlling the balance of political and military power. In Mexico they were practically synonymous. Eventually he had used them by conducting a revolution in favor of Pedraza, who thus got to serve three months of the four-year term he had coming to him.

Pedraza finally became *de facto* President toward the end of 1832, the year of the first outbreak of the Texian rebellion. He was a liberal, while Bustamente, who'd been in the saddle the past few years, was anything but that. He seems to have been particularly inimical to the Texians, who could have expected from him only the most savage retaliation. Their saving good fortune lay in his overthrow by Santa Anna just at this time.

In view of what was to come it is ironical that the colonists hailed Santa Anna's victory with a joy reaching beyond the facts that he had ousted Bustamente and had kept their pelts from being nailed to the door. As the man who had both saved Mexico from Spain and restored constitutional liberty to his country, he was looked upon as a high-minded patriot of the first water. A meeting of settlers passed a resolution giving Santa Anna a vote of confidence and promising support for his candidate in the forthcoming elections. Pedraza had been reduced to a figurehead, and one at the prow hardly long enough to get wet. Santa Anna was the embodiment of democratic hopes.

It was with a clear conscience, therefore, that John Austin could give assurances of loyalty to the commander of the Mexican flotilla which finally appeared at the mouth of the Brazos. Colonel Jose Mexia, the trouble shooter Santa Anna had dispatched to quell the Texian revolt, was able to report that the colonists had merely been anti-Bustamente and were enthusiastic supporters of the new regime.

That likewise proved to be the case with almost all East Texas garrison commanders, who led their forces south to

take part in the civil war that still raged in central Mexico.
The exception was Piedras, who remained loyal to the administration that had appointed him. The colonists had some
reason to respect him, but they weren't inclined to spare the
last of the garrisons which had tyrannized over them for so
long. As their ultimatum was ignored they closed in on
Nacogdoches. When, after some maneuvering, the garrison
surrendered and departed, there wasn't a Mexican soldier
left in the colonies. Exclusive of the garrison of the Alamo
there was none in all Texas.

The first phase of the rebellion had ended well, but that
wasn't enough for the colonists. Throughout the Texian Revolution, indeed, the resemblance to that of the American War
of Independence is noteworthy. The primary causes were
overtaxation and the absence of home rule. As most of the
Texians were the sons or grandsons of Revolutionary veterans it is not strange that they pursued a similar course in
struggling for their rights. At all events they did, alternating
violent resistance with formal appeals to a distant government that could not or would not see what they were talking
about. In this instance it was decided to follow up the success at arms with a request for separate statehood.

At a convention of settlers held at San Felipe de Austin—
not to be confused with the modern capital of Texas—what
was styled a "memorial" was drawn up and sent to the Mexican Congress. While stressing the loyalty of the colonists
toward their adopted country, this paper pointed out the
disadvantages to Texas of being yoked to Coahuila. Reminding the Congress that the Constitution of 1824 left the
door open for the old province to become a state in its own
right, the Memorial concluded by asking the creation and
admission to the Mexican Union of the State of Texas.

To add weight to their plea, and in an effort to keep the

petition from wearing the clothes of a strictly racial issue, the Texians had tried to enlist the support of the Mexican population. Exceptions allowed for, the Mexicans didn't fall in line, though, and the matter had to stand as one promulgated almost exclusively by transplanted foreigners.

It is not surprising under the circumstances that not only the authorities but Mexicans in general should have viewed the project with suspicion. Foreigners are acceptable when absorbed into the body politic, but when they act as a unit they are inevitably resented. Furthermore, the foreigners in question belonged to a nation which was believed to have designs upon Texas. It appeared to the Mexicans, to most of whom Texas was as unknown as Thibet, that the North Americans were inventing grievances for the purpose of starting trouble.

The petition was refused, but by the time the colonists received their answer things had happened which prevented the Texians from becoming too discouraged. Santa Anna had turned out to be his own candidate for president but had soon assumed the role of the man behind the scenes. Gomez Farias, Vice-President and acting President, was a vigorous and courageous liberal. In addition to passing measures which benefited the country as a whole, he rescinded the anti-immigration laws, once more permitting rapid growth of the colonies.

Elated, the settlers sent delegates to a second convention, held at San Felipe de Austin in 1833. At this one they went so far as to draft a constitution for the proposed State of Texas. Drawing up a new appeal to the Mexican federal government, they delegated Stephen Austin to take it to Mexico City.

Austin, who had always been a most conscientious and law-abiding citizen, proceeded to get himself into trouble.

He was well received by Farias, who, however, refused to consider the petition on the constitutional grounds of insufficient population, so he tried to enlist the support of Santa Anna himself.

Engaged in watching the reaction of the nation to Farias' liberal program, the president was gracious but non-committal. At length Austin lost his long stock of patience. In a letter to a Texian colleague he advocated forming a state organization without permission, trusting that a distracted government would accept an accomplished fact while it wouldn't take the trouble to act on a petition.

About then Santa Anna seemed to become more interested in the Memorial. He didn't promise anything, but he held out hope, provided Texas continued to grow. Much encouraged, the *empresario* started the journey home. He was well on his way when the police caught up with him and dragged him back to the capital. A Mexican official at Bexar, one of whose fads was steaming open letters, had read the one mentioned above and sent it to Santa Anna.

Apparently the only thing that saved Austin's life was that nobody in Mexico City could decide upon the exact nature of his offense and therefore just what court should have jurisdiction. These points were mooted for eighteen months before Santa Anna sprung him from prison, apparently believing that he was chastened and would preach resignation.

While he was enduring imprisonment, affairs were at first going exceptionally well in Texas. The new wave of immigration was bringing prosperity, a condition which always makes political mismanagement less noticeable. The colonists had been little bothered by either revenue collectors or military satraps since the outbreak in 1832. Furthermore the Coahuila-Texas legislature of 1834 had brought about some reforms. Texas had been granted a supreme court, another representative had been allotted, and so on. Things didn't look bad to the North Americans at all.

While they were arriving at that conclusion Santa Anna was forming some opinions of his own. By the spring of 1835, to be exact, he had concluded that the temper of the country at large would permit him to become a complete autocrat. Brushing Farias aside, he dissolved Congress and appointed stooges of his own to rule over the various states and important towns. In a word, he abolished the United States of Mexico, deprived the states of all autonomy and substituted for the old constitution one authorizing absolute central control. He himself, it need hardly be added, was the control authorized.

This wasn't accomplished all at once; the steps were taken cannily, over a period of months. Neither was it accomplished without opposition, yet Santa Anna not only controlled the army but was capable of leading it personally. The opposition either died, grew silent, or went elsewhere hurriedly.

Texas first got wind of the new trend when the recently passed liberal laws were wiped off the books by the more aggressive of the two legislatures, one seated at Saltillo and the other at the new capital of Monclova, which fought for control of the state. Even then most Texians still believed in Santa Anna and were confident that he would do something to help them. Disillusionment didn't begin to set in until political fugitives from Mexico proper began to arrive. Soon they had ominous confirmation of the reports these brought. Coahuila-Texas, its capital definitely moved back to Saltillo, was one of the states determined to retain its sovereignty; but a powerful force of government troops arrived to see that its legislature was dispersed.

Santa Anna had also developed plans for Texas itself. He had positively decided against permitting separate statehood, even of the farcical sort he countenanced. Instead he reinstituted rule by garrisons and revived burdensome tariffs to support them.

It was when this had been done that he allowed Stephen Austin to ease his way out of jail and to take the report of his failure back to the men who had sent him. The *empresario* was an angry and a troubled man. In the past he had always been the first to insist upon everybody's honoring the oath of loyalty to Mexico. He had always done everything in his power to have issues settled by peaceful means. This time he had a different message, although he refrained from using his influence to stampede others until the situation could be reviewed at a general consultation of colonists.

The Texians were by then all soberly aware of the crisis at hand. There had been trouble and new violence since the return of military force and customs control. John Austin had died of cholera two years before, but bold partisan leaders were seldom lacking on the frontier. There had been another incident at Anahuac, although one that didn't win popular support. A lot of heads had cooled since 1832. Most of the colonists wanted peace if they could have it and frowned on a reckless challenging of the government.

The split between factions of the colonists was actually almost as wide as the one which divided them all from the Mexican administration. What was patriotism to some was to others the antics of irresponsible adventurers who found swashbuckling pleasanter than work. There was a Peace party, still in the majority but weakening as refugees from Mexico City reported what was going on there, and there

AUSTIN'S MAP OF TEXAS IN 1835.

was a still small but resolute War party. Incidentally, they used precisely those names when referring to themselves or the opposition.

It was Stephen Austin's word that swung the balance of power to the War party when delegates representing all the colonies met upon his return from Mexico in September, 1835. As a former advocate of arbitration he carried all the more weight when he told them that in his opinion they would get no consideration from the current Mexican government unless they chose to fight for it.

He concluded his address by suggesting a committee whose obligation it would be to decide upon a course of action for the Texians as a body. This committee, he warned, would have only three courses to consider: to leave the country, to remain passive and accept whatever the government dished out, or to load guns while reasserting rights. His suggestion was adopted, and he himself was elected chairman of the committee charged with the heavy responsibility.

The decision was to resist at all costs the measures which were stifling the freedom and prosperity of the colonies. On October 5 a formal declaration of war was published in the committee's name; but by that time hostilities had already broken out, and Austin soon was on his way to take part.

Even before the delegates met there had been trouble at Gonzales, the nearest important North American town to the Mexican stronghold of Bexar. In 1831 this community had been presented with a cannon by the Mexican government. Its purpose was defense against Indian attack, but it had occurred to the Mexicans that it might now be used for other occasions.

Colonel Domingo Ugartechea, who had lost the fort at Velasco to John Austin back in 1832, had since been moved up to command the garrison of the Alamo. He sent a detachment to secure the field piece early in September, 1835, but the colonel had learned something in his years in Texas. He ordered his subordinate to be polite about it, and the captain charged with the mission was. He requested the return of the cannon which had been lent to the town of Gonzales. The citizens of that town were just as polite but pointed out that it had not been a loan but a gift, and one which they valued.

The debate continued, still on a more or less friendly basis. Meanwhile, the Texians had taken advantage of the captain's politeness to send into outlying districts for support. By the time the captain finally lost his temper and led his troops into town with intent to seize the piece, he found a sizable force of armed men flaunting a banner. The legend of the banner was "Come and Take It," which the Mexicans tried to do but couldn't.

At about that time Ugartechea was superseded by General Martin de Perfecto Cos, who landed at Matagorda with five hundred reinforcements for the Alamo garrison. Nothing could have been a clearer indication of the administration's intention of controlling the colonies. The new commander was not only military chief of the eastern states of Mexico but he was brother-in-law to Santa Anna.

Learning of the incident at Gonzales, Cos sent Ugartechea himself to capture the Gonzales field piece. Word of the expedition had reached the Texians, however, and they swarmed to the threatened town. What Cos had accomplished, indeed, was to crystallize a colonial army of which Austin was elected commander in chief. When Ugartechea observed the strength of the opposition he retired to Bexar without firing a shot.

The Texian army remained intact, however. Austin reached

Gonzales on October 10, and by October 12 the colonists had organized and made a decision to take the initiative. They struck out for Bexar, determined to break the Mexican grip on Texas where it was strongest. There were only a few hundred of them to begin with, but they moved slowly at first, picking up strength as more and more men rode out of the East to join up.

While this was going on the all-important question of just who was declaring war and under what circumstances was being decided at a consultation of colonial delegates at San Felipe de Austin. The previous temporary government had been a council composed of one member from each local committee of safety. This government was without a policy, and, in so far as it was a recognized makeshift, without official standing.

At the consultation it was decided first of all that the Mexican State of Texas, comprising the territory included in the old province of that name, was in revolt. Pending a future meeting of delegates it was to be ruled by a provisional government, and San Felipe de Austin was designated the temporary capital. As to the officials of the provisional government, one Henry Smith was appointed governor, James Robinson lieutenant-governor. The latter was also president of a board of fifteen elected councilmen, composing, with the governor, the two administrative divisions. General Sam Houston was appointed commander-in-chief to succeed Austin, who in turn was appointed a delegate to solicit aid from the United States.

Many of the colonists not only hoped for American assistance but were confident that the United States would jump at the chance to gain Texas by annexation. There was, however, nothing in the platform of the provisional government that indicated as much or even that it considered independence. The official status of Texas was declared to be that of a state which had temporarily withdrawn itself from Mexico in protest against the abolition of the Constitution of 1824 as well as against the adoption of centralized government.

Houston's appointment as commander-in-chief was effective immediately, but for more than one reason he did not immediately take the field. Even though he had been with the army in the beginning, the volunteers had elected Austin, and when Austin was gone they again wanted to choose their own commander. But these men had signed up for two months only; and after that period, organization on a more orthodox basis could begin. Houston laid his plans for a regular army and bided his time.

The first campaign, as it happened, was going very well without him. The garrisons at Goliad and Lepantitlan had been overcome, and by the end of October the main body of the Texian army had advanced to within a few miles of Bexar. On October 28 an important victory was scored at Concepcion Mission, on the eastern approach to the city, with the result that the old Texas capital was in a state of siege.

Not long afterward Austin's new orders caught up with him. The duties called for were more suitable to him than those of a general, so both he and the army were relieved. By election the command passed to Colonel Edward Burleson.

The make-up of the Texian army had changed considerably while it was in the field. The declaration of war had appealed to Southern frontiersmen, and volunteer units had come from several Southern states. Individuals and small groups from east of the Sabine were also arriving almost hourly. At its peak, the army enjoyed a comfortable superiority in numbers over Cos' eight hundred odd.

During the weeks the siege of Bexar lasted this advantage was lost. If new volunteers from the United States kept arriving, bona fide Texians were getting bored and went home to look after their farms and families in even greater numbers. An amateur army always shows up badly when it's marking time. This one finally dwindled until it numbered less than the force it was besieging. If Cos had been anything of a soldier he would have attacked; but he did nothing except send for more reinforcements.

What had made the Texians themselves hesitate to launch an assault was their chronic handicap, the lack of heavy ordnance. Still the majority of those left wanted to storm Bexar, and Burleson at length had the choice of having them do so with or without his approval. Colonel Ben Milam took actual charge of the attack which, though fatal to its leader, was successful. After most of San Antonio was taken in house to house fighting, Cos threw in the sponge without even trying to hold the Alamo.

Familiar with the sporting rules of war then often practiced, although not by Mexicans, Burleson freed Cos and his army on the General's word that he would not again take up arms against the colonists or in opposition to the Mexican Constitution of 1824. The Texians garrisoned the Alamo and were able to congratulate themselves that in two months they had cleared their newly created state of government troops.

IV

NEROS AT THEIR FIDDLING

NOW that a hundred and forty odd years have been run through as if they were week ends, it is necessary to slow down. The heart of the story is at hand. As promised, it begins on a note of absurdity, but that can wait a little longer.

First it is important to consider the geography and strategic situation of the colonies. They had been planned, be it remembered, to hold what had been the old Spanish frontier against the Indians. Roughly then they formed a hundred league arc stretching from the Gulf of Mexico, where the Nueces empties into it, to a point northwest of San Antonio.

Not all of the proposed grants had been taken up, however; not all of those which had been taken up had been well settled; and not all had been allotted to North Americans. There were a few small Mexicans colonies, and out of several efforts to settle Europeans one successful colony— the Irish one at San Patricio—had emerged. But it happened that most of the settlers from the United States lived north of the San Antonio River in a belt extending from the Gulf to the vicinity of Gonzales. The region is a coastal plain rising to hills six or seven hundred feet high. Its only natural defenses are the rivers which striate it. Running from northwest to southeast, these are the San Antonio, the Guadalupe, the Colorado, the Brazos, the Trinity and certain lesser streams. The coasts would have been vulnerable had the waters then been charted. As they were not, a fleet commander unwilling to risk wrecking his ships was forced to try the established ports. In the main they were guarded by captured Mexican fortresses.

San Felipe de Austin, the Texian capital, was a jerkwater town of two or three thousand located on the lower Brazos. If not the metropolis, it was as large as any in the colonies. The population of civilized Texas had been reckoned at twenty thousand in 1830. Illegal and then legitimate immigration had perhaps doubled it by 1835. The Irish had thrown in with the North Americans, but to estimate those sympathetic to the rebellion most of the Mexican population must be deducted. This amounted to some thousands.

The region had no industry or developed mineral wealth. The newly created state had practically nothing in the treasury. Unrecognized, it had no means of establishing international credit. To sum up, the Texians had neither man power nor resources, the two agents by which wars are commonly won.

Although kicked to pieces by years of civil war, Mexico seemed impossibly formidable by comparison. Periodic plagues, massacres and contested elections notwithstanding, the population ran into the millions. Mexico's resources, as then understood, had been developed for three hundred years. Compared with Texas it was industrially advanced. Mexico City, then as now, was one of the great cities of the New World. Financial resources, though badly strained, were present in quantity.

In this contest geography was a Mexican handicap upon which many Texians counted too heavily. The center of population was far south beyond the arid and rugged northern plateau. Only the southern portions of the great states just below the Rio Grande had been well settled, and there was only one town which amounted to anything on the river itself. As southern Texas had not been settled, there was an expanse of uninhabited country several hundred miles wide between the two hostile regions. The wretchedness of communications made supplying a large force difficult and costly; but these barrens had been traversed by troops before and could be again.

Weighing all the factors, it would appear that the Texians had only two points in their favor: There was the advantage of being able to lie back, making the enemy reach for them over great distances and unspeakable roads. And then, as a homogeneous group which had acted in successful harmony before, they could present a united front to a foe split by bloody feuds.

Repeat: these were the two highest counters on their side —and the Texians would have no part of either. Shortly after the taking of Bexar the cry was raised that the war should be carried to Mexico. And with a ridiculous completeness, hard to conceive of in view of the speed with which it took place, the brand-new State of Texas fell apart.

With the united colonists behind them the army had defeated Cos, sweeping the state free of Mexican troops, on December 10, 1835. A month later a people whose numbers scarcely justified one government were hearing conflicting orders from two.

The army was even richer in leadership. A force which, at top strength, would make only a couple of fair-sized battalions soon boasted four officers more or less recognized as commander in chief.

By these tokens the Texians had descended about as far into foolishness as a people could go. Yet the general conditions which made it easy for them to get bogged down in nonsense aren't hard to outline. It was hardly to be expected, for instance, that a coherent nation could be formed of disparate communities overnight. A country in swaddling clothes is as balky, intractable and messy as any other infant; and in Texas there were probably more reasons for failure to co-ordinate than in many other places.

Since the North Americans had arrived, their state had never had a government of its own, nor had it been even organized as an entity. Except for garrison control there had been little government save that of the respective grants and townships. These were isolated one from the other in a wilderness which had as yet hardly been scratched. Mail service was haphazard when existent. Newspapers were few and the problems of distribution painful. The only reliable means of communication was by a courier adroit enough to elude wandering Indians.

Another handicap was that everybody was a newcomer, more often than not of only two or three years' standing. There had, therefore, been a minimum of time for leadership to develop and for worth to be recognized. By the same token, the men put in authority had had, in some cases, scant experience in dealing with official colleagues. There was as little understanding of the responsibility toward constituents.

Most of the Texians were veteran frontiersmen, which is to say that their way of life forced individual competence, allowing little practice at being a cog in a machine. Political parties would have had a settling effect, making disagreement while preserving union a possibility; but the state had not been operating long enough to have evolved such impersonal vehicles for expressing opinion. Instead there was bitterness and faction.

Lastly, a new country, by creating opportunities, begets opportunism. A man can help his country with a full heart, but with an even fuller one if he's also helping himself. There were too many Texians who wanted to be high cockalorum, and being men of action they did something about it.

As far as the army was concerned folly also had a traceable genealogy. The Texians were backwoods farmers, and they couldn't be expected to have any concept of the endurance and patience demanded by organized warfare. They were willing to fight again later on if necessary, but just then they had other things to do. The campaign of 1835 had come at a relatively convenient time for them—neatly sandwiched between harvesting and spring planting—but the seasons wouldn't hold off while they hung around military posts. The men had taken care of all the war they could see and felt it was time to get back to work.

Even before the siege of Bexar was over many had left. The successful assault on the city released them all from any strong feeling of military responsibility. Moreover, they'd only signed up for two months, which was the exact duration of the campaign. Officers and men, the Texians climbed on their horses and went home, leaving word that they could be notified when needed.

Within a week or so after Bexar had fallen, the astonished and disgruntled volunteers from the United States found themselves the largest component of the army. Of the Texians proper only a minority remained under arms. Even Burleson, who had succeeded Austin in command of the army, had quit to attend to his own affairs.

With such conditions, civil and military, for fertilizer, trouble didn't take long to spring up. It began in the army. The American volunteers had come to fight, not to wait around for the Mexicans to return. Were it not for the fact that most of them had missed most of the fighting during the fall they might not have stayed at all. Even as it was they, too, were threatening to go home if something didn't happen soon. The Texians still in service expressed the same feeling.

A Dr. James Grant, who had served as aide to Burleson, was quick to exploit that mood. He had never been a Texian until he was pushed out of his extensive holdings in northern Mexico by the Santa Anna regime. He wanted to get his property back, and he thought he saw a way. Enlisting the support of Colonel F. W. Johnson, senior officer at Bexar after Burleson's departure, he launched propaganda booming that was known as the Matamoras Expedition.

Matamoras is in the northeast corner of Mexico, just across the Rio Grande from the present city of Brownsville. Before the American city grew up to overshadow it, it was the chief town of the lower valley. As a port it was strategically located, being the natural point for Mexico to land and send forth sea-borne supplies for an invasion of Texas. It had long been an important garrison town and was, indeed, the place where Cos had had his headquarters before he went to Texas. Seizing it looked like a sound maneuver.

For a larger, well-organized army it would probably have been a worth while venture to raid such a natural focal point for enemy strength. But the Texians didn't have the men to spare from their own defenses, and the army was no better organized than a centipede with jake leg. It developed that everybody who didn't want to go home wanted to go to Matamoras; and if a Texian private wanted to go some

place the only way an officer could lead him was to find
out where he was heading and get in front of him. The
officers were just as wilful, taking orders when they appealed
to them. The Matamoras idea, that of carrying the fight to
the enemy, appealed.

In political circles the expedition met with both strong
favor and intense disfavor. It served, in fact, to bring a
division of opinion on policy to the point where it became a
violent quarrel. Basically the difference was grounded in
the question as to whether or not complete independence
of Mexico should be declared. The factions backing each
had cogent arguments.

Those arguing for secession claimed that there was no
possibility of reconciliation with Mexico except upon Mexico's own unacceptable terms. Furthermore they pointed
out that until a declaration of independence had been published no help could be expected from the United States.
Those against secession said that the United States wouldn't
step in anyhow—in which they happened to be right—and
that the best bet was to collaborate with numerous but
unnamed Mexican liberals in a general movement to oust
Santa Anna. They were positive—albeit quite erroneously—
that the Mexicans as a whole were ready to revolt against
centralized government.

The Matamoras Expedition, promoted at this crucial stage
in discussion, presented each party with its first opportunity
for a stand on a specific act rather than on a general program. They chose opposite positions with a firmness soon
backed by anger and then virulence.

The side favoring continuance of the union with Mexico
liked the expedition because it was a step toward co-
operation with allied forces in Mexico. For a second string
to its bow this party made capital of the fact that it was

better to take the war out of Texas. The ones advocating independence did not want to collaborate with anybody in Mexico or to do anything else which might bind them to the parent country, and so were against marching upon Matamoras. Their secondary argument was the military impracticability of the undertaking.

As it chanced, Governor Henry Smith and his advisory council, the two divisions of the provisional government, were on different sides in the controversy. Smith was an old wheel-horse of the War party who had shown his sincerity by getting himself seriously wounded in the campaign of 1832. He was honest and capable in certain directions, but he lacked the patience which makes for political aptitude, and he didn't know how to disagree with men without showing he thought them rogues, fatheads or both.

He put up with what he considered the contumacy of his council for just so long, then he publicly blasted them. The council retaliated by impeaching him and then firing him. They had no authority whatever for such a procedure, but they did it and expected it to stick. Lieutenant-Governor James Robinson, designated acting Governor, conducted himself as if he were in truth the head of the state by the will of the people.

It would have simplified things if Smith had agreed that he was dismissed, but he carried on as a one-man government, threatening to shoot any councilman who tried to get hold of the state seal. Inevitably the two administrations directed at each other an energetic wrath that could better have been saved for the Mexicans. This is the stuff of broad farce; though even as comedy it was a failure due to the large measure of responsibility it bore for the disaster of the Alamo.

Instead of taking steps to close the breach, the people

took sides. But no vote was taken, no convention of delegates was assembled for the purpose of reorganizing the government. The quarrel dragged on while the problems of state defense went begging.

In part, at least, the electorate let it go because of overconfidence. Having done well with a pick-up team many thought victory was something they could have on their own terms. Others thought Mexico had learned its lesson and would be glad to make any concessions. Some thought it would be impossible for Santa Anna to send a force large enough to be dangerous across the Mexican deserts. Even those who expected invasion didn't expect it before spring, and spring seemed a long ways away. They let the councilmen do as they pleased.

In disagreeing with the Governor the council may or may not have been acting reasonably. Any revolution is a gamble, and only second guessing can see the difference between shrewd daring and foolhardiness. Certainly on one or two points they could just as easily have turned out to be right as wrong.

They could be granted a doubt concerning the business of deposing Smith and setting themselves up as a replacement government without a mandate from their constituents. They might have felt they were walking on the right side of the often slim line between treason and enterprising patriotism. But in their dealings with the army they were as criminally stupid as the Governor held them to be.

Typically, the decision to descend upon Matamoras had been made without consulting the Commander in Chief. Apprised of the undertaking, Houston gave it his limited approval only. He agreed that a hit-and-run raid would be a good idea, but he put his foot down against stripping the defenses of the state for an invasion he felt it would be

impossible to carry through. He likewise refused to leave
his work of organizing the new regular army to lead the expedition.

The council was not to be balked. Without notifying
Houston they gave most of his powers to Colonel F. W.
Johnson. Disturbed by the opposition of the Governor to the
Matamoras Expedition, Johnson refused; so the sweeping
military authority necessary was conferred on Colonel James
Fannin. Meanwhile Johnson decided that he'd lead the expedition after all. Without batting an eye or relieving Fannin of command, the council gave Johnson the requisite
orders. At about this time Dr. James Grant informed the
council that when Burleson had retired he had passed on
to Grant the position to which he'd been elected. The council recognized him as Commander in Chief of Volunteers.

Even before the council had absquatulated with the government and scrambled the chain of command, the state's
military situation had continued to deteriorate. Due to public indifference and the lack of official co-operation, the
army of regulars of which Houston dreamed remained a
skeleton. Among the volunteers and except for a few officers,
Texians were now conspicuous by their absence. As commander at Goliad, Fannin later complained that out of about
four hundred men only twenty-five were residents of the
state. The commander of the Alamo stated that his 104
men were nonresidents almost without exception. Most of
the disillusioned American volunteers would have left the
army, too, if they hadn't been broke.

Such was the force of which Sam Houston found himself
commander. He was the man the Texians needed, but why
they had sense enough to know it remains a mystery. They
could not have been censured had they passed him over.
Once they decided to use him it would have been more

logical, on the strength of the record, to find him in Smith's chair rather than at the head of the armed forces. In the United States he had been a national figure for a dozen years and had learned the taste first of fame then of notoriety. Now in his early forties, the best years he had known were well behind him.

Born in Virginia in 1793, Houston was raised on the extreme Tennessee frontier of the day, just across the Little Tennessee River from Cherokeeland. When his family decided that Sam, at the age of fifteen, should clerk in a store, he picked up his Homer and crossed the stream to join the Indians. When not memorizing the *Iliad* he lived as a savage, complete with costume or the lack of it, for three years.

His pro-redskin leanings didn't extend to all Indians, however, for at nineteen he served against the Creeks under Andrew Jackson (LL.D., Harvard, 1833). In his capacity of ensign he led a charge or so at the Horseshoe which netted him an arrow wound, a couple of bullet holes and Old Hickory's good opinion.

Following the Creek War came the War of 1812, which blended with it, and a couple of years of peacetime service. During the latter period Houston served as an Indian agent for his friends the Cherokees, acquiring a lasting influence over them. Admitted to the bar after his retirement from the army, he soon became a member of the House of Representatives. There he performed his duties with such distinction that the Jackson Democrats had no trouble in electing him Governor of Tennessee.

He took office as the state's chief executive in 1827. Two years later Jackson was President and Houston, who had made a good job of the governorship, was regarded as his heir apparent. Thus on the crest, he compounded his good fortune by marrying a lovely, socially prominent girl with whom he was completely infatuated—and within a few weeks he was washed up.

His wife left him, creating a national scandal upon which his political enemies fell with joy. Resigning his governorship, Houston rejoined the Cherokees, many of whom were by then living in northeastern Texas, was adopted into the tribe and became an Indian chief.

The quality of the man is shown by the fact that he never once talked either in his own defense or against his wife. Now it is believed that the breach followed his discovery that, far from returning his romantic affection, she had been dragooned into the match by her ambitious family. But the absence of an explanation left it a matter of editorial opinion; and in handling the lives of public figures newspapers were even less delicate and more imaginative than they are today.

Whatever the facts, Houston was politically ruined in the United States, and, though he did good work in his new position, several times saving the tribe from the voracity of Indian agents, being a Cherokee chief was hardly a compensation. Nor is it probable that the squaws he took to his wigwam gave him satisfactory heart balm. He had a fine, poetic Indian name; but in the course of time the Cherokees knew him more often and less formally as Big Drunk. It looked like complete disintegration.

So it was as a has-been, the odds against a comeback a hundred to one shot, that Houston came among the Texians in 1832. Jackson, with his extraordinary capacity for hating and liking, had never let go of him, even when he caned a pistol-packing Ohio congressman who had publicly questioned his honesty. As a matter of fact, the incident tickled Old Hickory, who gave it as his opinion that the manners of some other congressmen would profit by the same treatment.

It was a mission from Jackson which brought Houston to the Texas settlements, and many thought he remained there as Jackson's agent. That may have been so at first, for the President was interested in Texas; but Houston was soon involved in affairs on his own account. Undoubtedly he saw in the rebellious colonies a last chance to make an acceptable place for himself among his own kind again. Immigration was still banned at the time, but he stayed.

He had already made his way sufficiently to be designated a delegate to the colonial convention of 1833, the one which drew up the second petition to make Texas a separate state. By the fall of 1835 he had so won upon the colonists that he was appointed Commander in Chief of the army.

This was a lucky choice rather than one which made sense. Houston's military record, in the days when he was making one, was no more significant than that of any other young fireball who had played a very minor martial role with distinction. After the Creeks got through with him his health kept him in the rear echelon throughout the War of 1812. Three years after it he resigned his commission as a first lieutenant.

That was the extent of his practical military experience, and it had ended nearly twenty years before the Texas Revolution. True, he had been made a major general of state militia three years after leaving the army. Once a frontiersman got hold of a good title he held on to it, so he was still known as "general" while the best the rest of the prominent Texians could do—practically all of them had some sort of military title, barring a few known as "judge," "doctor" or "squire"—was to sport an honorary colonelcy. Yet the major-generalship had, if anything, less martial significance than his lieutenancy as a regular, and in any case he had forfeited it years ago.

Among the possible candidates there were a number whose military records were longer, more distinguished and more recent. There were those, for instance, who had played leading parts in the Texian campaigns to date, which Houston had not. But he got the appointment, and he was the right man. None of the other possible choices showed any comprehension of the terms upon which Mexico might be beaten.

Houston started in, however, by taking a beating himself. And it was the Texians he was supposed to command, not the Mexicans, who overwhelmed him.

In spite of the political malfaisance that was ruining the country, Mexico was, much more than has since been the case, something of a military power. The great martial tradition of old Spain had not yet died out when independence had been achieved only a dozen years before. All the senior officers had been trained in the European military tradition at a time when it had been brought to a high point of development by the Napoleonic wars. The Mexican army had been further strengthened by mercenaries, veterans of those wars. Besides an immense advantage in numbers it had four things lacking to the Texian army: organization, discipline, a system of training and a reasonable percentage of the weapons needed.

Having been a regular, Houston appreciated the enemy's strength and knew what he had to have to combat it. In spite of public apathy and an unco-operative council he was making some headway toward building an enduring organization when the problem of the Matamoras Expedition rose to bedevil him.

The General was naturally angered at hearing of the plan at secondhand, but he saw some merit in the idea. He had no intention of going himself, or of committing a large force;

but he was willing to order the undertaking, provided it was led by a man whose judgment he could trust. Behind this effort, transformed in his plans from a major invasion to a diversionary thrust, he intended to poise a force to meet Santa Anna's inevitable counterstroke.

Houston's choice of a leader was Colonel James Bowie, but the latter didn't receive the order, due to the fact that he had left Goliad for Bexar, until too late. In the meantime, the General got wind of the fact that plans for an invasion of Mexico were going ahead without him. Perforce he left his imperative staff work to try to quash the business by a personal appeal to the troops.

It was only then that he found out what he was up against in all its enormity. The split in the government was just taking place, but nobody had bothered to tell the General. Nor had he been in touch with the activities of the council. He had never found that body helpful, but apparently it hadn't occurred to him that its members would assume the authority to displace him. Then he found that they had given his powers to three men, none of them responsible to him or to each other. A logical mind contemplating such depths of unreason explodes. Houston's letter to Smith following this unusual discovery is worth reading.

The main concentrations of troops were at Refugio and Goliad; though Colonel Fannin had sent out word for all Texians to gather at San Felipe, and Colonel Johnson had published a manifesto urging all to assemble many leagues away at San Patricio. Dr. Grant, also a supreme commander of the expedition, continued to team up with Johnson. These last two didn't recognize Houston's authority at all, Johnson claiming that Houston had no jurisdiction over volunteers, but over regulars only. Fannin coolly told his general that he would obey him if he followed the orders of the council rather than of the Governor.

Finding his army stolen from him, Houston yet did the best he could, with qualified results. Unable to address the troops as their commander, he sought them out informally, trying to convince them that an attempt to invade Mexico would be disastrous to Texas. He dissuaded a considerable number, but plans for the expedition weren't given up. Perforce Houston left them to it and turned north, pondering his own course of action.

The General's first intimation of trouble from supposed subordinates had come from Bexar earlier in the month. Word had reached him that when Colonel Johnson and Dr. Grant had taken it upon themselves to promote the Matamoras Expedition they had looted the Alamo of ordnance and quartermaster supplies in addition to luring away the better part of the garrison. This had been a blow to Houston's plans second only to his subsequent discovery that his authority was being completely disregarded.

Although there was some settlement below it, the San Antonio River with its two anchoring forts at Bexar and Goliad was a reasonably strong natural line shielding most of the colonies. It was the one, indeed, where Houston had always counted on making his stand when Santa Anna attacked. But its effectiveness was dependent upon the maintenance of the two fortresses.

Now one of those strongholds had been seriously weakened in favor of the Matamoras Expedition. In the current state of Texian military affairs both men and supplies were irreplaceable.

It is commonly stated that Houston had already ordered the abandonment of Bexar before he made his abortive visits to Fannin and Johnson. But Houston not only indicates that, he indicates several other things. His letter of January 17, written to Governor Smith, just prior to his trip, seems to state that he had done so at one point, while at another it seems equally plain that he is leaving the decision up to the chief executive. However, his letter of January 30, also written to Smith but on the way back from his journey, contains the phrase: *should Bexar remain a military post, Goliad must be maintained.* Of a certainty that shows no decision had been made.

Now Houston, as he also stated, had been planning to go to Bexar to look the situation over personally when he was deterred by the need for trying to break up the Matamoras Expedition. In his letter of January 17 he told Smith that as long as he couldn't go himself he was sending a man whose prudence and foresight he prized. In other words, he wanted the opinion of a trusted subordinate, based on firsthand information, before giving up the historic gateway for the invasion of Texas.

Had the decision rested with the Governor or the General, all that would have been needed was a messenger bearing flat orders to Colonel Neill, commander at Bexar, who remained loyal to them both. Instead Houston sent a valued counselor with a detachment of reinforcements—supernumerary, it need hardly be pointed out, to a post that was surely going to be abandoned. On that man's shoulders rested the responsibility of advising as to whether or not Bexar should be evacuated and the Alamo blown up.

Part II

FOUR MEN REACH THE ALAMO

V

BOWIE

THE man Houston sent to Bexar was one whom the President of Mexico was most anxious to hang. He was Colonel James Bowie, wearer of the original knife of that name, and one of the great figures of the old Southwest who became legends while living.

He was born in Georgia, Tennessee, South Carolina or Kentucky, depending upon the biographical authority followed, and the year of his birth was between 1790 and 1805. Recent scholars have narrowed the range of his nativity to Georgia and Tennessee, the majority holding that his parents moved from the former state to the latter a few years before James was born. The year, it is now generally agreed, was 1795.

Bowie senior was a veteran of Marion's hit-and-run campaigns during the American Revolution. After it, he picked a bride out of a Savannah finishing school, taking her first to the Georgia frontier, then to the even wilder one of Tennessee. He was a good picker. Once when he was jailed for shooting a trespasser, the finishing school girl from Savannah smuggled in a couple of pistols; and when they walked out she was looking along the barrel of one of them. She also gave all her children a better than average education, grounding them in Latin and the classics of literature.

In 1802—and hardly anyone dissents from that date—the Bowies moved out of the United States, taking their half-dozen surviving children to the Spanish province of Louisiana. Specifically, they settled in what is now Catahoula Parish of the State of Louisiana, afterwards moving farther south to the vicinity of Opelousas. It was a region of small prairies, great swamps and vast forests. When made available for cultivation the land was extremely rich, and the Bowie plantation prospered. On it and around it James had a boyhood unusual even for the American border.

Although Louisiana became a part of the United States in 1803, French and to a lesser extent Spanish were more commonly heard in many parts of the state than English. Bowie grew up speaking and writing all three languages. It was a facility he never lost and one which profoundly affected his way of life.

A knowledge of languages, however, was merely incidental to his early environment. The neighboring Cajuns had been in the deep woods for a couple of generations, and the instinct of the Frenchman—the instinct that made the *voyageurs* and the *coureurs de bois*—was strong in them. The tendency of the Anglo-Celt was to tear down the wilderness. The tendency of the Frenchman was to merge with it. Cajun youngsters were as wild as Indians, but with a reckless élan all their own, and they taught the Bowie brothers some unusual diversions.

Among these were the roping and backing of alligators, the object being to spring on one of these great reptiles and to keep it from either submerging or biting the rider. Enjoyment of such a sport indicates a robust disposition as well as strength and agility. The Bowies were reputedly experts.

A more practical activity was running down the wild steers which inevitably abounded wherever Spain had placed settlements. Some used a lance for this type of hunting, but the Bowies used lassos, also a Spanish importation. The sport was to trip the steer and, before it could recover, spring to the ground, dash in and cut its throat. It should be borne in mind that these cattle were longhorns, cousin to the terrible ring bulls but toughened by living as wild animals. Their flesh was prized though, and in that part of the frontier it was a staple of diet.

Bowie thrived on it as on the life generally. He grew to be six feet one, weighing 180 pounds. His body was well proportioned and contained a dynamic strength, perfectly controlled. As for his looks, his hair was reddish brown, his eyes gray-blue, his complexion very fair. The testimony of his portraits is that he was not only handsome but fine looking. The face is intelligent, lively and strong. The expression tells of good temper.

Like most frontiersmen, Bowie was on his own before he had attained his full stature, starting a saw mill in partnership with two of his brothers. The venture was successful; but the big money in Louisiana was in the swiftly developing cane sugar industry, and the Bowies wanted a piece. As in the case of so many other profitable pursuits the hitch was that a man had to have money before he could qualify to make any. The brothers sold their saw mill and sought a swift means of pyramiding their profits.

Down on Galveston Island Lafitte and Campeachy were flourishing. Lafitte was a master of pirates and a fence for pirates; but as he supposedly limited his activities to Spanish shipping most Americans regarded him benevolently. It was fashionable to view him as the patriot who had helped to win the Battle of New Orleans, and to take his word for it that he was dedicated to the cause of Mexican liberty. Merchants from Boston, New York and Philadelphia, as well as from New Orleans, made no bones about dealing with him; and as Lafitte was too canny to trade in American territory they came to see him at his mansion, La Maison Rouge. Campeachy became a prosperous port as well as a buccaneers' rendezvous.

Of the many things Lafitte commandeered from Spanish ships in the Gulf the most valuable as well as the most difficult to cash in on were Negro slaves. The United States had a sternly enforced embargo against importing any more, and the pirate, who had already been caught off base while operating in American waters, would not engage in smuggling them himself.

As far as the landsmen of the old Southwest were concerned, the law against bringing in slaves worked about as well as any other act which doesn't have popular approval. Labor was the crying need of the frontier; and people who took slave ownership for granted saw no reason to distinguish between native-born and foreign Negroes. They bought slaves if they could get them, insisting only on the legitimacy of the sale.

The smuggler was provided with this legitimacy by the government itself. It was difficult to get Negroes into the United States, but once importation had been achieved, marketing was easy and wore a bow of official red tape by way of blessing. When slaves had been successfully introduced the first step was to notify the local customs officer that such a thing had taken place and that the Negroes had been discovered and rounded up. The customs representative then officially confiscated the slaves and—strictly following the law—auctioned them off to the first person willing to pay a reasonable price. This was the smuggler. The customs man then—also strictly complying with the law—rewarded the informer by paying him half of the money he had just given for the Negroes. This informer's reward was the smuggler's certain profit, less what he paid Lafitte. It was a foregone conclusion, however, that he could sell the slaves for more than he himself had bid for them.

That was the field of enterprise which the Bowie youngsters entered, using the profits from the saw mill as capital. It was on the initial trip to Campeachy that Bowie first saw Texas, though the coastal region could not then have shown him much to arouse his interest. Reminiscing years later, one of the Bowies mentioned that they left small boats at the inlet to Calcasieu Lake. Calcasieu Bayou was then the route by which they smuggled the slaves through the mighty Louisiana cypress swamps and into the plantation country. How they negotiated the coastal swamps that separated them from Texas after they left their boat isn't clear, but apparently they went overland to what is now called Port Bolivar. It was not a healthy country for more reasons than one. The Karankawas still enjoyed cannibalism and had recently dined on five of Lafitte's pirates who thought it would be fun to go on the mainland and catch a squaw. Nerve alone was not sufficient for such a journey; only men with a rich knowledge of woodcraft in general and the intricacies of swamps in particular could hope to be successful.

The Bowies made several trips and soon were able to ensconce their now widowed mother and a bride or so in a promising sugar plantation they named Arcadia. That was all two of them wanted from their dealings with Lafitte; but here the character of James becomes distinguishable from that of his brothers. He kept on after the necessity had disappeared. He wasn't especially interested in money; what he throve on was the excitement and the gamble.

It was while he was so engaged, making the perilous round trips to Campeachy with only one Negro retainer to help him, that Bowie got his first look at the interior of Texas. A wandering band of Indians picked up his entire group of contraband darkies, who'd tried to escape while he was resting. He trailed them west for a hundred miles in an effort to get them back singlehanded, but he was only indirectly rewarded for this vote of self-confidence. He finally lost the trail in a stretch of baked ground. Meanwhile he had seen a country which aroused his imagination.

The earliest manifestation of his interest was joining General James Long, whom he may have met at Campeachy, on one of that filibuster's attempts to take over Texas. As Lafitte came to Galveston Island in 1817 and Long made his attempted invasions in 1819, the date range for Bowie's connection with the Pirate of the Gulf can be limited if not fixed. The years that immediately followed are harder to tag.

He was at Natchez, at New Orleans, in Arkansas, in New York; he went on long hunting trips. In 1824 he is said to have been at Bexar in the course of a trading expedition. He may have made other such journeys to Texas; he seems always to have been on the go. The plantation was making plenty of money, and the Bowies operated the first steam sugar press in Louisiana; but Arcadia was only the beginning and ending of wayfaring for James. It was during these years, in the early and middle 1820s, that the Bowie legend was in the making.

As indispensable to his saga as the bow to that of Robin Hood is the Bowie knife. James made it the favorite side arm of the southwestern border, but it was his older brother who designed and first used it. There are extant a good half-dozen accounts of its forging left by men who personally knew the blacksmith who did the work—in each case a different blacksmith. But whoever he was, he was a craftsman of mark, who had, it is guaranteed, discovered the secret art of Damascus.

Rezin Pleasants Bowie had the weapon made following an accident on a hunting trip. When he'd rushed in for the kill after roping his steer his fingers slipped down the haft to be sliced open by the blade. Thus made dissatisfied with the one he had, he carved a model of what he conceived to be an ideal knife out of wood. This he turned over to a smith, together with a file of which to fashion it. The result was a knife with an eight and a quarter-inch, single-edged blade, an inch and a quarter wide. It had, of course, a guard.

Designed strictly as a hunting weapon, it wasn't used for anything else until James' pistol snapped when he was attempting to return the shot of a man who had fired at him. Worried by the circumstance, Rezin gave his prized knife to his brother, remarking that it would never fail him in a pinch.

Rezin always insisted that brother Jim never fought a duel in his life, although he did concede—and he had a nice choice of words—that James had used the blade betimes "in a chance medley, or rough fight, between himself and certain other individuals to whom he was then inimical." "Medley," though now seldom used in that sense, is a form of "melee" and exactly descriptive of the most notorious encounter in which the knife functioned. This was the famous battle of the seconds on the Natchez sand bar.

The numbers on each side range from five to twenty—choose your own authority—but there is no disagreement as to the basic facts of the action. The engagement did not start as a medley at all; it was a duel with an unusually large number of official supporters allotted to the principles. The reason for this is that they were burdened with the wrath of factions as well as their own. It followed that the seconds were mutually antagonistic, although they commenced by conducting themselves with the decorum called for by the rule books.

All would have gone well if one of the duellists had but nicked the other. As it happened, both missed, whereupon they composed their differences and prepared to leave the field in amity. That was more than the outraged seconds could bear. As the challenged and the challenger wouldn't fight, they made for each other. In a moment everybody, including the attendant surgeons, had been drawn into the medley.

Drawing a pistol to cover a threatened friend, Bowie was shot through the leg, then once again. It didn't take very long for single shot pistols to be emptied; after that it was war at close quarters. Bowie's leg had given way, leaving him stretched out on the ground, and an old enemy, a Major Norris Wright, rushed to take advantage of his situation. In his hand as he sprang forward, Norris held a sword he had drawn from his cane. It was then that Rezin's remark about the reliability of a knife wore the shape of prophecy. Both of Bowie's pistols were empty, but he drew the blade as he raised himself to meet the Major's attack. An instant later Wright was heard to groan: "Damn you, Bowie, you've killed me!" Crippled though its wielder was, the knife had been rammed home.

At the end of the fray there were barely enough able men left to carry the dead and to assist the wounded from the field. The affair made the other survivors marked men, but

it was only an incident in Bowie's career. He and the knife
had become bywords long before.

After James' demise the family maintained that he was a
peace-loving fellow. During his lifetime Big Jim himself,
who was the reverse of a braggart, never talked about his
exploits. But the Bowies were the only ones who did not
profess to know of his adventures. Accounts of his activities
began to be standard newspaper copy. Everybody, at first
in the Southwest, then in a larger orbit, had heard of him
and knew remarkable stories about him.

Bowie developed a mystical trust in his blade, and there
was reason for it. Once it was the death of three desperadoes
who had jumped him simultaneously. He became so sure of
it, on the other hand, that he could afford to be merciful.
After crippling the knife hand of Bloody Sturdivant, the
arrogant river gambler, he spared him.

There were others who, for one reason or another, he did
not spare. He fought standing in a small circle, his left
wrist tied to that of his opponent. The man who backed from
the circle declared himself a craven; but the option of retreat
wasn't always given. At least once Bowie fought when the
buckskin breeches worn by both his foe and himself were
nailed to the log on which they were seated. On another
occasion the log spanned a stream. His antagonist was a
Mexican who put his faith in a poniard, and though no
nails were used the left wrists were tied. Bowie needed but
two motions, the first to pierce his man and the second to
slash the thongs which bound him to the corpse. The stream
carried off the body.

Bowie did not invariably fight with his knife, however,
and was not always shackled when he did. He shot John
Lafitte, the Pirate of the Gulf's son, in a duel on a Mississippi
paddle boat. And he and a Creole buck, both barefooted,

entered an unlit room one night in New Orleans. The Creole with a sword, Bowie with the knife, they sought opposite sides of the room, to steal in search of each other when a signal was given from without. The knife found a place for itself in the Creole.

Then there were numerous spontaneous encounters, not to mention those which didn't take place because the party of the second part thought better of it when he learned who Bowie was. Yet it is noteworthy that Bowie was never reported as the real aggressor. In most instances, indeed, he didn't fight on his own account at all, but rather to protect or avenge some helpless third party. For example he once went to hear a sermon and found that the preacher was being heckled so loudly and persistently that he could hardly make himself heard. At length James rose and observed that if there was any further misconduct he'd take care of it by cutting off the wind of the offender. "I'm Jim Bowie," he concluded; and thereafter the minister had a model congregation.

To seek the character of the man in the stories told about him they should be compared with those which concern the other two men of the old Southwest who became legendary while alive. Nothing of the same spirit was related about Mike Fink or Davy Crockett.

To begin with Fink, there was never an attempt to imply that he fought out of anything but a savage desire to crush his opponent. If Fink was heroic, he was a heroic gouger of eyes, a heroic river bully. Even the cruel facets of his domestic life weren't scamped. Piecing together the Fink saga, the reader can have no doubt that although the old Southwest had a gusty appreciation of the man known as the Snag and the Snapping Turtle, it appraised him realistically.

Unmistakably differentiated again are the tales told about

Crockett, like Fink a rough-and-tumble artist. Davy didn't fight as often as the others, and when he did it was generally out of a high-spirited desire to prove physical prowess. He was presented, usually, in fantastic terms, but the hyperbole wasn't so thick a haze as to hide the portrait.

The stories told about Bowie, then, are an exposition of how the men who knew him felt about him; and such direct commentary as has been preserved bears them out. Bowie is invariably described by his contemporaries as an unassuming, courteous man, provoked into using his remarkable capabilities only when his sense of propriety—granted, a touchy one—was outraged.

An interesting passage about him is contained in a letter by that charming and knowledgeable memorialist, William H. Sparks. He knew the Bowies well and was a neighbor of Rezin's at the time of the fall of the Alamo. Rezin he describes as a man of unusual mental and cultural attainments. He even goes so far as to compare his social discourse to the disadvantage of Sargent S. Prentiss, the Admirable Crichton of the day. James he describes as a normally well-educated gentleman of assured social bearing, noted for keeping his word and being faithful alike in his dealings with friends and enemies. While not of the same distinguished mental caliber as his brother he was possessed of an unmatched physical alertness. Sparks, who knew everyone, claimed that he was the coolest man in the clutch of any on the frontier and that he possessed a genius for finding clutches to be cool in. It should be added that in the opinion of most historians the old southwestern border was the roughest in United States history.

The statements of Sparks and others draw attention to the peculiar diversity in Bowie's way of life. The sundry American frontiers have known many deadly bravos, but most of them were professional scouts, professional badmen or professional hunters of badmen. Almost all of them, too, were either illiterate or a bare cut above it.

Bowie was a man of property and, when he wanted to be, a capable businessman. He was at home in the woods, but he was equally at home with the established society of old cities like Natchez. He knew how to get along in an Indian village or among the punctilious upper-class creoles of New Orleans or San Antonio. Most dangerous men are apt to be either men of no control or men of limited emotion; men who are passionate lechers or drinkers, or men possessed of an abnormal asceticism. Bowie astonishes investigation by his soundness. He was self-controlled but warmhearted; he drank but he had other things to do; he got along with women but he was no skirt chaser.

It was with his reputation and his capacities at their fullest development that he permanently settled in Texas in 1828. The Bowie knife was not yet, as was later to be the case, manufactured in England for the American frontier trade. Nevertheless, it had already been widely copied by individuals. The old Southwest recognized it as a superior combination of hunting and fighting knife. The man who carried the original was a man of mark even in Mexico long before he came to live there.

Bowie did not settle among the North American colonists on any of the land grants. Had the developing of a plantation been his interest he would have stayed in Louisiana where the sugar holdings of which he was part owner were producing a very comfortable annual income. He did not come to Texas to be a farmer, and he took up residence in Bexar.

Originally he was attracted by the possibilities for land speculation, a business activity at which he was by then no tyro. Some years before he had been associated with a group of men, including his older brother John, in extensive land deals in Arkansas. The titles under which the land was sold were called in question, but the Superior Court vindicated the Bowies and their colleagues. Four years later, under pressure from the United States government, the titles were voided, but by that time Bowie had sold all his holdings. There have been efforts to prove Bowie was culpable. The facts are that at the time he was willing to meet the challenge of the law and was upheld by it.

Of course, land speculating, like stock speculating, is a gambler's pursuit, which is why Bowie liked it. He did well at it in Texas where his familiarity with Spanish was very useful. Gambler or not, he was welcomed at Bexar. As noted, he had the faculty, not reserved for all Americans, of getting along with Mexicans.

The laws of Mexico demanded that anybody who hoped to make a living there had to become a citizen. As a heretic could not receive citizenship, acceptance of Roman Catholicism was a necessary preparation. The change of religion and nationality disturbed Bowie no more than it did the rest of the Texians; but he had an inducement most of them did not. Soon after reaching San Antonio he had fallen in love with Ursula Veramendi, the beautiful young daughter of the very wealthy Lieutenant-Governor of Coahuila-Texas.

On the frontier it was unusual for an eligible bachelor to stay in that category until his middle thirties, but Bowie had done so. He knew what he wanted when he saw Señorita Veramendi, though, and he sweated out the protracted courtship upon which Spanish custom insisted. He was married in 1830 and, with the exception of one activity, settled down.

From the early days of Spanish colonization there had

been reports of marvelously rich silver mines near the site of the old San Saba Mission, 150 miles northwest of Bexar. The ancient archives of Mexico affirm the existence of such mines, though at a somewhat different location. Due to the difficulty of the undertaking no immediate attempt was made to exploit them, and then it was too late. The map giving the exact location had been stolen or lost.

Efforts had since been made to relocate the mine or mines, but there were serious obstacles to exploration, some called Apaches and others Comanches. They didn't want white men looking for the treasure; yet they had a tantalizing habit of coming into Bexar wearing new silver ornaments. Fact or legend, the story of the mines couldn't sleep while that went on, and neither could many men who heard about it.

Looking for lost wealth while outwitting guardian savages was the sort of thing to appeal to Big Jim; he had to try for it. In order to have a free hand for exploration he spent months hunting and fighting side by side with the Apaches. He became so popular that he was adopted into the tribe; then suddenly he was asked to leave the tribal lands. Bowie always thought the Apaches had discovered he was on the trail of the mines. He also thought he knew where they were, or perhaps he had actually seen the fabulous lode. His contemporaries believed that he had.

At any rate upon his return to Bexar he sent for Rezin. He and his brother gathered a party totaling, themselves included, eleven. Setting out in November, 1831, they were around a day's journey short of the old mission and the nearby ruin of the fortress of San Luis de las Amarillas when a friendly Comanche warned them they were being trailed by a large party of Caddos looking for scalps. Unable to reach the fort, they holed up in a little grove of trees.

In the upshot, it was one of the most notable stands in the history of the continent. The Caddo war party numbered 164; but the marksmanship of the treasure hunters was deadly, and they had made skillful use of the undergrowth and rocks to provide themselves with concealment and cover. After a fight that lasted for fourteen hours the Indians called it quits and withdrew. The Bowies withdrew also, not thinking it prudent to penetrate farther into a country so aroused against them.

In his official report to the Jefe Politico of Bexar, Bowie estimated that Indian casualties ran into the thirties. It wasn't until some Comanches rode into Bexar a few days later that all the returns were in. These Comanches had come upon the Caddo war party at its mourning ceremony. They had counted fifty corpses, not to mention thirty-five who were merely wounded. The Bowies had lost one man, while three others were wounded.

By intention Bowie wasn't through with the mines, which have ever since been called after him, but he was soon absorbed in the Texian revolt of 1832. The North Americans, having captured Velasco and declared for Santa Anna, were set on ridding their territory of all garrisons. At Nacogdoches Colonel Piedras still maintained his allegiance to the old government, and the colonists attacked. Unable to hold the town, Piedras attempted a westward withdrawal only to find himself cut off by a Texian cavalry detachment. In command of the detachment was Colonel James Bowie. Like most other frontiersmen of note he had somehow collected a military title.

With only twenty men Bowie had made a swift ride around the Mexicans and was waiting for them when the point of their column rode into a stream which coursed through a gulch. When the Texians fired the Mexicans retreated, Piedras resigned his leadership, and the new commander ran up the white flag. By the time the main body of the colonists had caught up, Bowie had accepted the surrender of the Nacogdoches garrison, 310 men in all.

He was next prominent as a delegate to the Colonial Convention of 1833, the one which drew up the second memorial requesting statehood. As the local government at Bexar was either not sympathetic or was unwilling to be thought sympathetic to the actions of the North Americans, it appears that Bowie attended more or less on his own. Certainly he couldn't have represented much of a constituency.

In this connection it should be pointed out that of all the Texians Bowie had the most to lose and the least to gain by taking part in the revolt. He was not a colonist and did not have a status separate from that of a native Mexican citizen. His social and business interests were focused in Mexican communities—Bexar in Texas, Monclova and Saltillo in Coahuila; and as a land speculator he was peculiarly dependent upon the good will of Mexican officials. Moreover, the special taxes and punitive measures which afflicted the other North Americans did not affect him. The cities where he maintained homes were not subjected to garrison rule, and, if the Mexican laws were not too liberal, an in-law of the influential Veramendis was a privileged character.

Not long after the convention of 1833, however, his closest tie with Mexico was severed by cholera. Ursula Bowie died of it under circumstances that must have caused her husband extra anguish. There was a great outbreak of the plague in Mexico that year, and it was feared that Bexar would be hard hit. It was believed that the mountainous country of Coahuila would be much healthier, and Bowie had an estate in the vicinity of Monclova. Although he remained at Bexar, at his insistence his wife went south; and there the plague found her and the two Bowie children, an infant boy and girl.

Bowie took it hard. His first reaction was to leave Texas permanently and, forfeiting his vast land holdings, he went to the United States to find what solace he could with his family. By the next year he had returned, however, to engage in speculation on an even more heroic scale.

It was at this time that the capital of Coahuila-Texas was shifted from Saltillo to Monclova. The Mexican, Menchacha, makes the interesting statement that Bowie engineered the shift. Whether that was so or not, the legislature, operating from its new stand, made a stupendous amount of Texas acres available for exploitation by speculators. Bowie, it goes without saying, got his slice. As had been the case in Arkansas, he had only done what the law permitted, but the transactions stirred the enmity of conservative Texians.

Unlike many of his critics, however, Bowie was always ready to put business aside in favor of graver matters. By the middle of 1835 Santa Anna had pretty well shown his hand. There had as yet been no formal talk of declaring war; but there were rumors of Mexican strength concentrated at Matamoras for the purpose of crushing Texas before the North Americans could start anything. Nobody could ascertain what, if anything, lay behind these rumors, so Bowie went to find out.

Disguising himself as a Mexican, he rode into the garrison town and spent some days taking inventory. He was personally known to a large number of bona fide Mexicans and might well have run across one who would recognize him. Nevertheless, assisted by his command of vernacular Spanish, he got away with it. As a result of his espionage the Texians knew in advance just when and where Cos would land and how many troops he would lead on the march to Bexar.

This information was of value to the War party in its fight for a united opposition.

When the War party won ascendance, and the Texian army came into being at Gonzales, Bowie was taken on as a volunteer aide, a position carrying the honorary title of "colonel." In the ensuing campaign he distinguished himself in two engagements.

The first of these was the Battle of Concepcion, named after the old mission just outside of Bexar where it took place. Bowie, assisted by the then Captain Fannin, was in command of a reconnoitering detachment of some ninety Texians. The heavy mists of dawn in a river valley enabled a force of over four hundred Mexicans to draw near before either side was aware of the other's proximity. What took place can best be followed by excerpts from Bowie's report to his commander, General Stephen Austin. If it isn't a model military communication it is both graphic and explicit:

The face of the plain in our front was nearly level, and the timbered land adjoining it formed two sides of a triangle, both of which were as nearly equal as possible; and, with the exception of two places, a considerable bluff of from six to ten feet sudden fall to our rear, and a bottom of 50 to 100 yards to the river.

We divided the command into divisions, and occupied each side of the triangle for the encampment on the night of the 27th, Captain Fannin's company being under cover on the south side, forming the first division, Captains Coleman, Goheen, and Bennett's companies (making in all only forty-one, rank and file) occupied the north side, under the immediate command of myself, (James Bowie, as aide de camp) . . .

. . . When the fog rose it was apparent to all that we were surrounded, and a desperate fight was inevitable, all communication with the main army being cut off. Immediate preparations were made by extending our right flank first division to the south, and placing the second division on the left, on the same side, so that they might be enabled to rake the enemy's lines should they charge into the angle, and prevent the effects of a cross-fire of our own men, and at the same time be in a compact body contiguous to each other, that either might reinforce the other, at the shortest notice . . . The men, in the mean time, were ordered to clear away bushes and vines . . . and at steepest places to cut steps for a foot-hold, in order to afford them space to form and pass, and at suitable intervals ascend the bluff, discharge their pieces, and fall back to re-load. The work was not completed to our wish, before the infantry were seen to advance, with arms trailed, to the right of the first division, and form the line of battle at about 200 yards distance from the right flank . . .

In this manner the engagement commenced at about the hour of eight o'clock, A.M., on Wednesday, 28th of October, by the deadly crack of a rifle from the extreme right. The engagement was immediately general. The discharge from the enemy was one continuous blaze of fire, whilst that from our lines was more slowly delivered, but with good aim and deadly effect, each man, retiring under cover of the hill and timber, to give place to others while he reloaded. The battle had not lasted ten minutes, before a brass double fortified four-pounder was opened on our lines with a heavy discharge of grape and canister, at the distance of about eighty yards from the right flank of the first division, and a charge sounded. But the cannon was cleared, as if by magic, and a check put to the charge . . . "The cannon and victory" was truly the war-cry, and they only fired it five times, and it had been three times cleared, and their charge as often broken, before a disorderly and precipitate retreat was sounded, and most readily obeyed, leaving to the victors their cannon.

Thus a small detachment of ninety-two men gained a most decisive victory over the main army of the central government, being at least four to one, with the loss of only one brave soldier, and none wounded; whilst the enemy suffered in killed and wounded near 100, from the best information we can gather, which is entitled to credit, say sixty-seven killed . . .

No invidious distinction can be drawn between any officer or private on this occasion. Every man was a soldier and did his duty, agreeable to the situation and circumstances under which he was placed. . . .

The only thing left out of that report was the fact, cited by others, that Bowie personally led the charge to seize the cannon. Successful, it was the turning point in the battle.

It was this defeat, involving about half the Mexican garrison, which convinced General Cos that he'd better stay in Bexar instead of chancing an all-out encounter with the entire Texian army. In the course of the siege which followed, the famous Grass Fight took place.

Erastus Smith, so called by his parents, but known to everyone else by his soubriquet of "Deaf," was the first of a long line of distinguished Texas scouts. He was nearly as silent as he was hard of hearing, but when he said he saw something nobody ever doubted him. At Bexar his orders were to keep watch for attempts to reinforce the garrison, as it was known that Colonel Ugartechea had been sent south for that purpose; but there was an additional possibility that made his duty interesting.

Captured Mexicans had stated that pay for all Texas garrisons—including several which the Texians had just liquidated—was on the way from the other side of the Rio Grande. Mexican soldiers were paid in hard silver, so quite a train of pack animals was expected. Therefore when Deaf Smith saw a long parade of loaded mules even his bad ears could hear the coins chinking, and he spurred back to headquarters with the word.

For such a call it was inevitable that Bowie should be on hand and the first in the saddle. Rounding up sixty riders, he sped away while the main attacking force was being organized. On the plains south of Bexar he intercepted the mules and their protecting cavalry. The latter outnumbered the Texians, but Bowie dismounted his men and turned them into snipers. To keep from being plain targets for expert riflemen, the Mexicans perforce dismounted, too, and were held pinned down, pending the arrival of the Texian main body.

The action had occurred, however, in plain sight of Bexar, and help for the mule escort was on the scene before the other North Americans. Nevertheless, Bowie succeeded in holding both Mexican forces, at the same time keeping the mules from being led away. The coming of Texians in strength decided the engagement but only after some sharp skirmishing. The Mexicans still able to do so left, and the mules stayed. It is to be hoped that they were good mules, for like Cophetua's bride they could be prized for themselves alone. Instead of silver they were laden with bundles of forage for the hungry mounts of the beleaguered garrison.

It is written both that Bowie played a distinguished part in the storming of Bexar and that he played no part at all because he'd been assigned to other duties. Certainly he wasn't one of the division leaders. But, whether Bowie was present or not, and in spite of the fact that Cos did eventually receive strong reinforcements, Bexar was surrendered. The Alamo was at last in the hands of the Texians and was garrisoned with about four hundred men.

One of the great weaknesses of an amateur army is that it has no program in the event of victory. At the conclusion of the campaign General Burleson, who had succeeded Austin, set the pace by giving himself a vacation from the war. In the course of a few weeks most of the Texians proper had done likewise. Those who remained in service were divided in allegiance by dissension over policies, so that in the end Houston had only a handful of adherents. Of this small group Bowie was one.

Yet in spite of a record of service as distinguished as any in the Texian army, Bowie couldn't get a regular commission. Houston tried for him and had to confess failure. The council had been given the authority for granting commissions, and the council simply shelved all requests relative to Bowie. In part this was owing to the fact that the members of that body and their political backers had never forgiven him for his land speculating as authorized by the Monclova legislature. More influential probably was the very fact that he was known to have the commander in chief's approval.

Meanwhile Bowie wasn't standing around with his thumb in his mouth. In the three weeks which followed the fall of Bexar a succession of missions took him to Copano on the Gulf, to San Felipe on the Brazos, to Goliad, back to Bexar and so to San Felipe again, where he arrived January 1, 1836. A couple of weeks before Houston had wanted him to head the Matamoras Expedition, but due to Bowie's activity the message was long in catching up with him. By the time it did, Bowie had learned from Mexican sources that the Matamoras garrison had been greatly strengthened, so the plan was dropped.

On this visit to the Texian capital Bowie secured the authority to raise a regiment of volunteers, which meant that he still had no place in the regular army. He had started on this thankless assignment and had enlisted thirty or so men when the harried Houston learned of the spoliation of the Alamo by Johnson and Grant.

In view of his inability to strengthen the garrison, the General questioned the advisability of maintainng the post at all. He seriously considered having the Alamo blown up, but he wanted the on-the-spot opinion of a man whose judgment he could trust. He sent Bowie, who promptly took off, his volunteers in train. Leaving Goliad January 17, they arrived at Bexar on the 19th.

Bowie took his time to arrive at a conclusion, and he had reasons. The situation was undoubtedly bad. Lieutenant

Colonel Joseph C. Neill, in command at the Alamo, had only 104 men in place of the thousand it would take to garrison the fort adequately. Of those remaining, most were discouraged because they had never received their promised payment and some had already sold their rifles for drinking money. Nevertheless Bowie decided in favor of holding on. Neill, arguing the difficulty of abandoning the Alamo, reported that he didn't have mules and horses enough to salvage the fort's cannon, which the Texians could ill afford to give up. Bowie had stronger words to offer.

His report to Houston is not in the record, but a letter to Governor Smith, written on February 2, gives his position:

The salvation of Texas depends in great measure on keeping Bexar out of the hands of the enemy. It stands on the frontier picquet guard, and if it was in the possession of Santa Anna, there is no stronghold from which to repel him in his march to the Sabine. Colonel Neill and myself have come to the solemn resolution that we will rather die in these ditches than give them up to the enemy.

VI

TRAVIS

UNLIKE Bowie, who preceded him, or Crockett, who was to follow him into the Alamo, William Barret Travis had no claim to fame aside from his part in the Texas War of Independence. But with that revolution he was dramatically identified from its very beginning to its tragic fourth act. His destiny was bound up with it and, to the extent that a man can be, he was aware of it. His letters relative to the subject all bear a conviction of dedication.

By some accounts he was born in Alabama or North Carolina, but majority opinion holds that he was a South Carolinian. The date of his nativity is given as 1809 or 1811, with most votes and the probabilities in favor of the earlier year. At all events he attended an academy in South Carolina but left without graduating. Significantly his departure from school was due to a student revolt, in which he took an aggressive part, against a tyrannical administration. Soon after the incident he left for Alabama, read for the law and was admitted to the bar.

Unfortunately the portrait of Travis which has been offered cannot, owing to discrepancies in costume, be accepted as his, and the authentic sketch doesn't tell too much. A description of him has been handed down, though, which is startlingly like that given of Bowie. Like the latter he had red in his hair, blue-gray eyes, and a fair complexion. At six feet he was one inch shorter than Bowie, and at 175 pounds he was five pounds lighter.

Those who hold that Travis was not a frontiersman born can find support in his thinking. He was essentially a traditionalist, a man who backed the old, profound moralities of honor, dignity and loyalty with an unabashed rhetoric worthy of America's founding fathers. That much of him showed the influence of the old South of the Atlantic seaboard; but withal, he was an experienced frontiersman and had learned to appreciate frontier improvisation before he even thought of going to Texas.

Although the United States border had moved west of Mississippi when Travis came to Alabama in the late 1820s, that state still had all the earmarks of a border territory. Mobile was an old town, but neither the French, British nor Spanish, successive owners of the region, had settled the interior. On the whole it had been noticed by white men less than any other state east of the Mississippi prior to 1800. Even then immigration was discouraged by two geographical facts. More than half of the state was in the possession of hostile Creeks, Cherokees and Chickasaws; and the Gulf coast still belonged to Spain, hampering export in a land dependent upon rivers to the sea.

The War of 1812 served to remove both these handicaps. Andrew Jackson crushed the Creeks with a thoroughness that made the other tribes amenable to treaties, and General Wilkinson, doing something constructive for perhaps the only time in his career, took Mobile away from the Spanish.

Alabama became a state in 1819, but complete settlement only came with the boom cotton prices of the late 1820s and the 1830s.

The life of the young lawyers who flourished in this exuberant period of growth has been preserved by Joseph Glover Baldwin in that superb American classic, *Flush Times of Alabama and Mississippi*. It was a paradise for youthful professionals, for, as Baldwin points out: "In the new country, there are no seniors: the bar is all Young America. If the old fogies come in, they must stand in the class with the rest, if, indeed, they do not 'go foot.' "

They started at the top and in consequence had an unrestrained faith in their powers. They did not have to defer to precedent, they created it. They were leading citizens of the state, socially elect, marked for political preferment, and they made sufficient money. It was youth having its way in the world to a degree not elsewhere possible, and paradoxically it matured them early. In the absence of older men they were grave toward responsibility.

At the same time they led a rough and ready life. Courts were separated one from the other by great forests. The means of travel was horseback, and the roads were bad even for that. There were many streams and few bridges. Every man was a hunter and a woodsman.

Organized law enforcement was ineffectual in towns and nonexistent between them. Every man went armed, and another glance at Baldwin will show why this was the part of discretion: "And such a criminal docket! What country could boast more largely of its crimes? . . . What more terrific murders! What more gorgeous bank robberies! . . . Such McGregor-like levies of blackmail, individual and corporate! Such expert transfers of balances to undiscovered bournes! Such august defalcations! . . ."

Travis might never have left a region so excellently suited to a young man of his craft had he not concluded to sever relations with his wife in 1831. The details have never been revealed, but he had reason to suspect her of unfaithfulness, something that it was not in his nature either to wink at or forgive. He left his very comfortable bank balance and his daughter with his wife, took custody of his son and went to Texas. Divorce proceedings followed this move; but though his wife promptly remarried, Travis remained a grass widower.

As the Mexican law against immigration was then in force he could not become a citizen. Nevertheless, he took up residence in Austin's grant, settling at Anahuac and resuming the practice of law, quite undisturbed by the fact that he had entered the country illegally. In this he was not only acting the frontiersman but reflecting the attitude of most North Americans, who thought all Texas was theirs *de jure* and East Texas theirs *de facto*.

He seems to have done reasonably well, but for more than one cause Texas was not the happy hunting ground for young American lawyers that Alabama had been. Texas then had no courts of higher jurisdiction. To attain any real prominence at the bar fluency in Spanish was necessary, and even that was not too much help to a colonist. Eminence was vested in experienced Mexican barristers well known to the superior courts in far away Saltillo.

This reefing of his sails must have galled a man so recently accustomed to free coursing. Undoubtedly, too, Mexican court procedure, with its closed sessions and juryless trials, outraged him, as a lawyer, more even than it did most Americans. He was ripe for revolt almost from the moment he hung out his shingle; and revolt was ripe for him.

The year before he entered the country the anti-North

American immigration law had been instituted, and tariffs had been raised to a ruinous level. More or less simultaneously the colonists had been afflicted with a string of garrisons manned by an arrogant, quarrelsome soldiery. All this had been going on just long enough to have become a festering aggravation when Travis arrived.

To speed the action, it chanced that when choosing a town in which to settle he had hit upon the one where conditions were more unbearable than anywhere else in the colonies. Oddly enough, the most vindictive persecutor of the Texians was Colonel Juan Bradburn, christened John in his native United States. He seems to have taken delight in galling his former fellow-countrymen; and if he did not actually encourage his men to acts of lawless violence he did nothing to restrain them. On his own part he had laid violent hands on civil rule, throwing the alcalde of a town called Liberty into the calaboose, and arbitrarily moved the seat of local government to Anahuac, where he could keep an eye on activities. The blood of the colonists was at full boil over this condition of affairs when five of Bradburn's soldiers amused themselves by gang-raping a settler's wife.

Travis, in that April of 1832, hadn't been in the country much over a year, but he engineered the act of reprisal which began the first phase of the Texas War of Independence. What he did was not a lawyer's method of procedure, but Bradburn had shut that door to social arbitration in his own face. There was no authority from whom either civil or martial redress could be sought; and the rule of the frontier was that if a man was unable to do what was best he should do what he could. Travis organized a group of fourteen men and laid for the rapists.

Some claim that the first man they got their hands on wasn't one of the offenders at all. Mayhap the enraged colonists didn't look too closely. They had a Mexican soldier, and the object was to show all Mexican soldiers that the civil rights of North Americans had better be respected. Without bothering to move out of town they proceeded to tar and feather their victim.

They were applying this object lesson when Bradburn, to whom word of the incident had been brought, arrived to interrupt. Following an exchange of shots the vigilantes submitted to arrest. Other colonists were for attempting a rescue, but Bradburn ordered his men to place the prisoners between themselves and the guns of the North Americans. Travis urged his compatriots to shoot anyhow. They refrained, and he was hauled off to Anahuac Fortress.

There might have been no explosive follow-up but for Bradburn's ensuing actions. In the first place he refused to turn his prisoners over to civil authorities. Declaring martial law for the district, he said the prisoners would be sent to some Mexican tribunal for trial. That was tantamount to a death sentence. In the second place, when the colonists had captured a detachment of garrison troops and released them on the promise of an exchange of prisoners, Bradburn reneged.

It was this last act which ruined all chance of a peaceful settlement. Not the men of Anahuac only, but the Texians as a whole were soon in revolt; and the immediate issue was the disposition of William Barret Travis and his men.

It was then that John Austin led the way to Brazoria to get the cannon necessary to the storming of Anahuac's fort. Taking Velasco Fortress so that they could slip the schooner bearing the cannon past its guns, they were about to sail against Anahuac when Colonel Piedras fell into their hands. This time arrangements for an exchange of prisoners worked equably, and Travis was released unscathed.

Whether he brought the nickname with him from Alabama or whether he earned it after crossing the Sabine, he was known to his fellow Texians as Buck. Possibly it was at this time that he was first called by a name so suggestive of friendly admiration. At any rate, the proponents of liberty now marked him as a man to be counted on, while Mexican officials, taking a dimmer view, marked Buck Travis as a man to be watched.

In the Battle of Nacogdoches, in which the garrison of that town was captured later in 1832, he almost certainly took part, though the spotlight fell upon others. Provedly he was a consistent advocate of separate statehood in the years of comparative peace that ensued. He was, in fact, an advocate of so aggressive a policy that the conservative majority came to look upon him askance.

By the end of 1833 and throughout 1834 the conservative attitude that time would take care of injustice was winning strong support from the course of events. The hated anti-immigration law was repealed. There had been no attempt to reinstate garrison control of the colonies. The burdensome tariffs and taxes seem to have remained on the books; but nobody cared very much, for they weren't collected. Only Stephen Austin, rotting in a Mexican prison, suggested Mexican hostility, and fifteen hundred miles kept him separate from public attention. Furthermore, there was general prosperity, the arch-enemy of rebels. Extremists like Travis had to growl pretty low in their throats.

But in 1835, when Santa Anna began his drive for the dictatorship, the liberals came to life, this time as a group demanding that Mexico be given an ultimatum instead of more petitions. In a short while, the lines became sharply drawn between the War party and the Peace party. As usual the position of each appeared outrageous to the other; and as usual the Peace party was not so peaceful that it didn't want to do drastic things to the men who opposed it. There was a stalemate of bad feeling.

As once before, it was Travis who started things moving. This time he made an even more direct challenge to governmental authority than he had flaunted in 1832. The scene was again Anahuac where a detachment of Mexican soldiers was once again stationed for the purpose of enforcing the collection of sky-high customs duties. After observing the activities of this force for as long as he could stand it, Travis organized a company of volunteers, was elected its captain and declared his own war. In ambush he got the drop on the whole detachment, disarmed the soldiers and ran them out of town.

This time Travis fell far short of being a popular hero. The majority of the Texians still favored bettering their lot by talking things over. Although they'd revolted once before they felt that only Mexico's preoccupation with civil war at the time had saved them from a prolonged struggle if not out and out defeat. Austin had not yet brought back his damning report of conditions in the capital, and many had genuine hopes that Santa Anna would listen to reason. Others saw only that armed resistance would draw a more brutal tyranny upon them. Travis was condemned as a dangerous irresponsible, and it was publicly suggested that he should be turned over to the Mexican military authorities from whom he had once been delivered.

Although Travis had strong supporters, the censure was so loud and general that he was moved to publish a defense of his action in the newspapers. It was a belligerent counterattack rather than an apology, the statement of a man who felt that he had taken the only course open to a patriot. Congenitally he was impatient of all compromise with principle; yet he was not the sort of man to wash his hands of his fellows. In a letter to Bowie he wrote:

> The truth is the people are much divided here. The Peace party, as they style themselves, I believe are the strongest and make the most noise. . . . There is now no doubt that a central government will be established. What will Texas do in that case? Dr. J. H. C. Miller, and Chambers, from Gonzales, are I believe, for unqualified submission. I don't know the minds of the people upon the subject, but had they a bold and determined leader I am inclined to think they would kick against it. General Cos writes that he wants to be at peace with us; and he appears disposed to cajole and soothe us. Ugartechea does the same. God knows what we are to do! I am determined, for one, to go with my countrymen: "right or wrong, sink or swim, live or die, survive or perish," I am with them.

His largeness of mind was not shared by the Texians he had named. There was a plot cooked up by certain citizens of Gonzales to sell aggressive members of the War party to the Mexicans in the name of peace. Colonel Ugartechea, who seemed "disposed to cajole and soothe" the colonists had made out a list of proscribed men. Travis, of course, was on it; in fact he was perhaps the one whom the authorities were most anxious to get their hands on.

The name of Travis connected with a new overt incident at Anahuac naturally had an ominous ring to the ears of Mexican officialdom. The young lawyer from South Carolina had in effect restarted the revolution he had begun in 1832. His action had jostled all Texians out of complacence and made them think where they stood. His action, too, was a decisive factor in the determination of Mexican policy. It was at this time that Santa Anna first voiced his decision to overrun the colonies. Meanwhile he planned to place a saddle of garrisons on Texas that could not be shaken off.

Aside from witnessing signs of this intent, the North Americans had bad news from the south brought by Lorenzo de Zavala, later the first vice-president of Texas, and other political refugees. These had found that there was no place in Mexico for a live man who disagreed with Santa Anna. Among other things, they brought positive information that state government would soon be written off the books, that the Constitution of 1824 was being scrapped, and that Santa Anna was dictating a new one which would legalize all his oppressive acts.

Such information caused a realignment of the Texians, the War party strengthening though still in the minority. Many discounted the news as propaganda invented by Santa Anna's political enemies. More were waiting for Austin, now released from prison, to return and report before they committed themselves.

A severe handicap to Texian unity was the almost total absence of communication with the rest of Mexico. Civil intercourse was slight, and such official dispatches as came to Texas from other parts of the country normally went no farther than Bexar. The colonists really never knew what the Mexicans were up to until they were hit over the head.

Yet after months of shilly-shallying, unity became a fact overnight. Austin's return dovetailed with the efforts to seize the Gonzales cannon and Cos' arrival at the Alamo with strong reinforcements. The Peace party dissolved as such, and Travis' stock was up again.

When Austin took the field, Travis' self-promoted captaincy was taken at its face value. With that rank he served as chief of the army's scouts throughout the campaign of 1835. In the course of the siege of Bexar he proved his right to this position. Despairing of being able to feed his cavalry mounts after the Grass Fight, Cos decided to send a hundred or so to safe pasturage in the Rio Grande Valley. The horses, complete with a guard, made a dash for it, but the captain of scouts was on the alert. He captured the party, men and mounts.

During the storming of the town Travis was cited, without much elaboration, as having distinguished himself under fire. After Bexar's capitulation, however, he, no more than Bowie, remained as a member of the Alamo's garrison. He, too, went east to see what he could do for himself in the way of military advancement.

Unlike Bowie, Travis was successful. While he was loyal to Houston as the duly appointed Commander in Chief of the army, he did not have the disadvantage of being, as Bowie was, a man Houston had particularly singled out for promotion. Also Travis, as a colonist, had political influence which Bowie, more or less of an outsider, lacked. The council that turned the Colonel down not only gave the Captain a regular commission but raised him two notches.

He was first offered an assignment in the artillery but rejected it, asking and receiving one in the cavalry. As the Texians had no artillery to speak of, his preference was understandable, but history made it ironic. Horses were mainly just boarders at the Alamo, while the guns played a big part there.

As a lieutenant-colonel in the cavalry, his first assignment was to be in charge of recruiting the new professional army called for by the war plans of the state. Midway in his efforts, however, the breach between Governor Smith and the council became a chasm. In effect, the split was a new fissure between the old War and Peace parties. All Texians were now committed to fighting, but there was bitter argument as to whether the ultimate goal was the independence for which the Governor called or the better terms with Mexico upon which the council insisted.

There could be no question as to where Travis, always impatient of halfway measures, stood in this quarrel. And in this instance loyalty to a person as well as to an ideal was involved. During the years when the War party had been vainly urging a showdown with Mexico, he had conceived a great friendship for Henry Smith. This did not waver when the Governor's power was curtailed by civil dissension. Without heeding the siren calls to Matamoras, he stuck at his job of finding men for Houston's army.

Along about then Houston was finding out for himself, through his visit to the troops in the field, that he didn't have any army. On his way back he failed to think of any way of regaining control of the situation. He decided then that he would best serve the state by withdrawing from active operations until, when, as and if he was given genuine military authority. The provisional government had shown its inability to function, but plans called for a meeting, set for March 1, 1836, of delegates authorized to form a permanent government. Writing to Smith, the General asked for leave of absence until then.

At the time no decision as to whether or not the Alamo should be destroyed had yet been reached. On January 27, the day before he granted Houston's leave, Henry Smith answered appeals from Neill by sending reinforcements to Bexar.

In his current straits Smith couldn't give orders to many officers with an assurance that he would be obeyed. An exception was Lieutenant-Colonel William Barret Travis. Smith relieved him from recruiting duty and ordered him to the Alamo, along with all the troops he could round up.

Travis was not happy about the assignment. At hand were only about thirty men, hardly an impressive command, as he pointed out, for a field-grade officer. Lieutenant-Colonel Neill, in charge at the Alamo, ranked him by a number or so, and Travis saw no military luster in connection with being second in command of a dinky garrison. He wrote Smith two letters in an effort to get out of going; but he finally took the road on January 29. Not breaking his neck, he reached Bexar February 3.

Because of Bowie's conclusion that Bexar should be held at all costs, the Alamo still stood when Travis arrived, but it was pretty much of an empty shell. The reinforcements that had so far checked in were inadequate and nothing had been done about the depleted ordnance and quartermaster supplies. The main activity of the garrison was finding some means of passing the time.

The first break in the monotony was furnished by Colonel Neill. He may have shared Bowie's determination, as the latter insisted in his passionate report, "to die in these ditches" if necessary; but he thought he'd take time out first. In the casual frontier fashion he relieved himself of command on February 11 so that he could go home. He had received word that his family wasn't well.

Now the difference between an amateur officer who is receiving no pay, nor is likely to, and an amateur officer who gives his services for nothing may not be clear to an outsider. It was clear to the men who had received regular commissions in the all but nonexistent Texian army. Neill was anxious to surrender his post, but he did not pass it to Bowie who, though senior in rank, experience and age, was only a volunteer. In Travis, however, he recognized a peer, and to him he handed over the command.

At this point the volunteers asserted themselves. It had

been the custom in the Texian army for the men to have a voice as to who should succeed a retiring commander. This was a practice on which the newly made regulars understandably frowned; but it was the frontier way of doing things, and the volunteers were strongly in the majority. The men of the Alamo insisted on their rights, or perhaps that's too mild a word. It has been stated that they threatened to kill Neill if he didn't get in line. At all events he consented to having the vote taken.

If the garrison had been mostly composed of colonists Travis, as one of them, might have been sustained. A large percentage of the volunteers, however, were outlanders from various of the Southern states of the U.S.A. Travis wasn't known to them, but Bowie's mighty reputation had been familiar to them for years. When the poll was taken, therefore, they voted to ratify Bowie's colonelcy, making him the ranking officer.

Travis was disgusted, both with reason and without. On his side was the fact that Neill, assuming the traditional prerogative of a commander, had appointed him as his successor. On the other hand, Bowie had held more important posts during the fall campaign and in general had a right to consider himself better qualified.

In point of fact they were two remarkable men, both capable in emergencies, both extraordinarily sure of themselves, where only one was needed. Their correspondence shows that the two had previously been on friendly terms, if nothing more, but there was inevitable hard feeling over the situation confronting them. Travis was ardent and ambitious of winning distinction, feeling the weight of his thwarted capacities. Bowie was irked by the treatment he had received from Texian politicians and was in no mood to yield to the pretensions of the so-called regulars.

The former's first impulse was to leave Bexar when the command was denied him, but he briefly thought better of it. The dew was still on him as a professional warrior, but respect for the military tradition was native to the old South, where he had been educated. He had been given orders and, unlike many another frontiersman, he obeyed orders whether he liked them or not. Travis wrote indignantly to Smith outlining conditions at Bexar, but he stayed.

His primary complaint was directed against Bowie, whom he accused of being roaring drunk. This does not jibe with other statements about Bowie, which describe him as a moderate and controlled drinker, though there is some indication that he had used his cups to fill the gaps in action since his wife died. Of course, a man with only a reasonable amount of liquor under his belt can seem mightily drunk to anyone not so enjoying himself. Also an amount of drinking condonable in a friend can become violent overindulgence in an enemy. Perhaps it was so, and no doubt it looked so to Travis, who was an honest man, albeit riled and redheaded.

Travis also stated that Bowie had taken it upon himself to release certain prisoners duly sentenced by the civil authorities at Bexar. It was Travis' opinion that this would serve to alienate the good will of the townsmen. That was a logical conclusion, but it may not have been a fact. Other reports show that Bowie, more than any other Texian, had consistently striven to win the Mexicans of the state over. Bexar was Bowie's own stamping ground, and unlike most of the Texians he had lived among Mexicans, knew them and liked them. Aware that Mexican officials in Bexar could not be counted on, he may have been trying to create a favorable feeling toward the garrison among the populace at large.

If his purpose was indeed to secure local supporters it largely failed. In spite of the efforts of himself and other far-seeing North Americans, the revolution remained tied up with nationality instead of being an issue argued strictly on its political merits. The colonists were for separate statehood, if not more than that, and were willing to fight for it. The average Texas Mexican didn't feel so strongly about statehood, and if he was going to fight at all he'd much rather fight North Americans than his own people. In Texas and out, Mexicans suspected that the movement was all along what it later became—a step toward a declaration of independence. They were naturally opposed to a course which would expatriate them, leaving them a foreign minority where they had formerly possessed the advantage of being part of a native majority.

These were valid objections but not such as strong opinion honors. The colonists, having been mistreated by the Mexican government and Mexican soldiers, were not disposed to think well at any price of the people in whose country they had come to live. When these failed to join in a war against tyranny, the Texians placed the reluctance to the score of cowardice. Neither could see the point of view of the other, and time didn't sweeten misliking. There were a few Mexicans in the garrison of the Alamo; but in general it could be said that, though many acted friendly enough, every Mexican in Bexar was a potential enemy.

The conduct of the garrison probably did little to win friends to the cause of revolution. The Texians and their allies from the States, like soldiers since the beginning of armies, didn't devote their free time to manly exercise or the pursuit of some constructive hobby. Unlike the soldiers of most armies, however, they were off duty most of the time. They were in the war to fight, and any hour they weren't actually being shot at they considered their own. They were only at the Alamo when they could find no other place to eat or sleep.

Bowie has been criticized for not putting them to work readying the Alamo for a siege instead of letting them loaf. Possibly he was to blame; more probably he knew the men under him too well to believe they would accept any fatigue details. Probably he felt he was in luck because they stayed around at all, considering how bored they were. Commentators have remarked that the Texians, which is to say American frontiersmen, were the best of soldiers in a fight and the worst conceivable in the lulls between battles.

If the men had no cares but their own entertainment their leaders were not quite so indifferent to the future. To close the gap between regulars and volunteers, which had split the garrison—and as he had the upper hand, Bowie must have been responsible for the rapprochement—Bowie and Travis composed their differences. Although the former retained the edge of seniority, they recognized each other as co-commanders, both signing all orders and dispatches thereafter. That compromise had been arrived at, as a joint letter to Smith proves, by February 14, only three days after Neill left.

What had inspired this move toward unification was the persistent rumor that Santa Anna was sending a punitive expedition into Texas. Or to be exact there was the usual multitude of conflicting wartime rumors dealing with the subject. Santa Anna was either sending an expedition or was leading it himself, it was either coming overland or by ship from Vera Cruz, it was coming right away or it wouldn't arrive until the following summer.

Travis and Bowie both firmly believed there would be an invasion and that they would find themselves in its path.

Travis put his hunch on record in a letter, giving the middle of March as the earliest date on which the Mexicans might be expected. His reasoning was based on the theory that an invasion would be in retaliation for Cos' defeat and therefore its organization could not have begun before the middle of December. What he did not know was that Santa Anna had been making his plans since the preceding June. The capture of Bexar merely served to speed up preparations which had been going on all fall.

Reports concerning these preparations, as already stated, had come up from the south in profusion, but they were all discounted. It is the nature of rumors that one with a sound basis of fact appears no more probable than one with no basis at all. After listening to just so many the Texians put no faith in anyone's talk.

The delay was maddening to both men of impatience, but the unmilitary fashion of awaiting a hostile army disturbed Travis most. Once he had become co-commander he tried manfully to get the garrison to drill and work. The regulars obliged halfheartedly until they found that the volunteers continued to hold formations in the cantinas. They quit and the *status quo* was resumed.

There was some work done on the fortress at the last; repairs and improvements, it is mentioned, were under the supervision of Major G. B. Jameson, the garrison engineer. In general only the officers could be persuaded to do any work, however, so progress was slow.

But if the Alamo wasn't being strengthened very rapidly, its importance was growing in swift proportion to the deterioration of affairs throughout Texas. Before Travis arrived the seriousness of the situation was appreciated by the officers at Bexar. On January 26, a manifesto, signed by both Bowie and Neill, had been drawn up which proclaimed the garrison's loyalty to Smith and censured the council for causing a breach in the state. By way of emphasizing the need for unity it was superscribed: *from the Army in the Field.*

It was a vain gesture, as every word from East Texas told them. Political chaos increased. The army continued to dissolve. The Matamoras Expedition was bogging down. The opposition offered no other substitute for the crippled war plans of Houston. What it all added up to was that if the Alamo wasn't held there was nothing to keep an invading force from driving in from the west and overrunning the colonies.

Though the co-commanders fumed in a vacuum of boredom, time was running out. On February 19, a friendly Mexican brought assurance that he personally had seen thousands of troops in the process of crossing the Rio Grande at Laredo, but the Texians thought the report of a piece with other rumors. This one happened to be a fact.

Only a torrential rainfall, the truth is, saved the garrison from being bagged before they knew what was going on. The vanguard of the Mexican army had reached the Medina, only eight miles south of Bexar, on February 22 and were set for a swoop on the town when the rain bogged them down. Anybody who has had to do with Texas gumbo will know what the frustrated Mexicans were up against. It was absolutely impossible for them to move forward until the next day.

While the invaders were cursing the mud, the Texians, as it chanced, were enjoying themselves at a fandango. In his reminiscences Menchacha, who was present at the dance, has written what happened. A messenger handed Bowie a note apprising him of the proximity of the Mexican cavalry. Bowie called to Travis and with some difficulty persuaded him to leave the señorita he was with. Travis was temporarily in the spirit of mañana and told Bowie not to bother him with business when he had a pretty girl on his hands. His colleague insisted on having his attention, nevertheless, and Travis, too, examined the warning.

The information was so incredible that although both were worried they couldn't bring themselves to accept it; but they didn't have long to wait for confirmation. Early in the morning certain Mexicans, who had also been tipped off, started to get out of town.

The withdrawal of the garrison from billets in San Antonio to the Alamo, just across the river to the east, was accomplished by 8:00 A.M. on February 23. A guard posted in the cathedral tower finally announced he saw horsemen to the south; but when others, ascending to the lookout, failed to observe anything, skepticism began to prevail again.

Having spent the hours till dawn at the fandango, most of the men didn't feel up to reconnaissance duty, but two who were in better shape volunteered. Oddly, both of these, through the accident of having been sent elsewhere, survived the Alamo siege. John W. Smith unfortunately left no record, but Dr. John Sutherland was later to write the only eyewitness account of what took place just before the Alamo was invested.

The scouts didn't have to go very far before they heard orders being given in Spanish. Peering from a patch of woods, they saw a considerable body of cavalry drawn up in formation. An officer was riding along the front rank, talking as he went; apparently the troops were being given their final instructions before advancing upon Bexar. Both the men and their mounts were beautifully equipped, Sutherland noted, adding the interesting information that their polished armor gleamed in the sun.

The Texians didn't waste much time in observation, but, as they were dashing back to report, Sutherland's horse skidded on a slick of mud created by the rain of the day before and fell with him. The doctor's leg was pinned under his mount, but with Smith's aid he got free and raced on to give the portentous news.

The Texians, who had done so little while others would have been busy preparing for disaster, now did everything in a situation where most men would have found it expedient to run. Travis was in his element, and Bowie came to life. The bored loafers of the garrison became grimly efficient soldiers. The houses of fleeing Mexicans were ransacked for stores and abandoned cattle were rounded up and driven into the confines of the fort. Earthworks within the walls were thrown up and cannon were emplaced.

It was while this furious work was going on that Travis' destiny became manifest. Helping in the terrific task of mounting a cannon on a platform by hand, Bowie suffered a fall which shook him up very badly. Before he could throw off the shock he commenced running a fever, and the next day, being the second of the battle, he could hardly stand.

Mrs. Horace Alsbury, who was in the fort for at least eight or nine days of the conflict, stated that the malady was typhoid pneumonia. Others have guessed tuberculosis and plain pneumonia. The latter seems most likely.

In any case, Bowie realized he was in no condition to continue in charge of a fortress in a state of siege. Calling the garrison together, he informed them that from that moment on Travis was sole commander of the Alamo.

VII

CROCKETT

THERE is order and logic to the events which led Bowie and Travis to the Alamo. David Crockett's advent, which took place on February 11—the day Neill resigned command of the fort—might as well be ascribed to the dramatic sense of his guiding demon. He was not a Texian; he had not, indeed, ever set foot in the state until a month or so beforehand. He hadn't been sent by anybody, nor had he been stranded in Bexar by the fortunes of war as had most of the other volunteers from the United States. To all intents and purposes he simply meandered from Tennessee to the Alamo, arriving there in the nick of action.

Crockett, like Bowie, was a living legend; one, furthermore, that had already jumped the borders of the remarkable into the unshackled realm of myth. He was a national and an international figure, the inspiration of a whole school of hacks, and the godfather of America's most purely indigenous literary movement. He was also, and above all, the apotheosis of frontiersmen.

As he took thought to set down the facts himself, the

question marks which hover over the vital statistics of Travis and Bowie don't haunt the date and place of his birth. He was born on August 17, 1786, where the Limestone joins the Nolichucky River in Greene County, Tennessee. His father, a veteran of King's Mountain, had been born on the boat which took his grandmother from Ireland. Assisted by his Maryland-born wife, he kept a tavern on what had been the extreme frontier of North Carolina. Statehood for Tennessee was ten years away, however, and there is some question as to whether Crockett was born in the United States at all. Nolichucky Jack Sevier and his frontier cohorts maintained their own separate government in 1786 and knew the region as the State of Franklin.

Like most border youngsters, he was expected to find food for the pot as soon as he was able to drag a rifle into the woods surrounding the log hostelry. Crockett was a capable hunter at the age of nine. By his own reckoning he was an independent citizen at thirteen, for at that age he struck out for himself twice. On the second occasion he was gone for three years, eventually working his way as far east as Baltimore.

His early departure from home was owing to a row with his father, but when he returned to find that parent loaded down with debts, he farmed himself out for a year to help pay them off. Having taken care of that obligation he felt ready for bigger ones, and it is to this impulse that he owed his only formal education. A girl he wanted to marry refused to wed an ignoramus, so Crockett started scratching a slate at the age of eighteen. Unmoved by this gesture, his inamorata, without bothering to tell him that they were no longer engaged, married somebody else. Crockett called it quits at a half-year of schooling, and within a year or so had a wife anyhow.

His portrait shows him to have been a well-favored man, big beaked and with high cheekbones after the manner of the wilderness-born. The hair was brown, the eyes blue or gray, the complexion florid. He was upward of six feet tall and weighed, in middle life, something over 180.

In the years of his young manhood the border was moving west through the forest, and Crockett moved with it, first to Franklin, then to Lincoln, then to Giles, all of them middle Tennessee counties contiguous to Alabama. Before he had pulled up and planted his stakes that many times, however, he had served under Andrew Jackson, just as Houston did, in the Creek campaign of 1813. He was a scout and played his part with courage and distinction, but when he got tired of the war he—simply and frontiersman-like—went home.

That began and ended his active military experience prior to the Texas Revolution, though he had the usual association with the militia, vague as to detail but productive of much rank. Aside from his brief period of soldiering he did nothing for quite a few years but engage in the sufficiently rough business of being a pioneer.

As his constant shifting about demonstrates he belonged to the wild breed of pioneers that would much rather see new country than stay and develop it. The men who stayed where he had been became, many of them, prosperous planters. Crockett remained a backwoodsman. He supported his family, increased by three children, by doing a little farming in the tiny clearings beside the succession of small cabins he built, and he did a great deal of hunting and trapping. His method of acquiring new property was to move onto it.

It was a community of fellow-squatters in Giles County which launched him into politics. As yet unrecognized by the state, and anxious for some degree of law and order, they elected Crockett a magistrate. His ignorance of legal theory was then absolute, and he had probably never even heard of most of the state statutes. Unperturbed by such handicaps, he handed down decisions based on a legal code of his own and was able to boast later that his judgments were never appealed or resented.

His constituents were so favorably impressed that they sent him to the state legislature in 1821 and 1823. Subsequently he served two terms in the Congressional House of Representatives, then, following a defeat, one term more. It was a second defeat in 1835 that made him forswear politics.

Somewhere along the line he buried his first wife, acquired another, added to his flock of children and moved to northwestern Tennessee. Somewhere along the line, too, he had either acquired a little property or his wife had learned to get along without him. A visit to his family following his last unsuccessful election campaign convinced him that they were not in need of his immediate care. He therefore felt free to devote himself to the cause of independence in Texas.

Those were the bones of his life. Except for the early trip to the East and the belated entry into politics it was the normal life of a Southern backwoodsman. That was hazardous enough, what with its encounters with floods, the forest and wild animals; but he engaged in no really spectacular adventures. His political experience was limited and led to no pinnacles. Yet in his own day and ever since he has roosted high in the American pantheon.

In his case distinction was gained by personality rather than by achievement. He was a superb marksman and a mighty hunter. One season he killed over a hundred bears, slaying with his knife where the rifle ball had failed. But it was in a land where most men had these skills in a marked degree, and greatness stood only a fine hair taller than the average. His overwhelming margin lay in the facts that men were overjoyed by his company and that he had the gift of gab.

Much has been written about backwoods balladry, but the frontiersman's characteristic form of artistic expression was not the ballad but the prose episode. As in all interesting episodes, they were compounded of strict factuality. If the facts sometimes seemed unusual it was up to the raconteur to show by a weaving of circumstantial logic that it could not have happened otherwise.

At this brand of saga Crockett was the acknowledged champion. In a world of skillful woodsmen he held the place of honor around the fire which cooked his kill. He was likable and liked people. He was a brave in the border tradition, a tall husky able to hold his own with a jug, or with any man in a rough and tumble fight. The tales he told were not appropriated by his hearers but clung around him. Other men when they felt called upon to make the marvelous credible began to speak not of themselves but of Davy Crockett.

His skill with the rifle came in time to be a by-word among the very animals he hunted. One shrewd raccoon, when it found Crockett's sights swinging in line toward him, was known to have cried: "Don't shoot, Davy; I'll come down!" Later Crockett developed a faculty which saved bullets without relying upon the common sense of raccoons. He could so daunt them by the confidence of his grin that they'd drop from the tree willynilly. This was but the beginning of his reputation, then confined to his own forest bailiwick.

Some historians claim that he owed his political career,

too, to his ability to tell yarns; and if so he wasn't the first or the last elected for that reason. Nevertheless, he had done well as a magistrate, thereby underlining an important facet of his character. He was much more than a politician with a knack for making buffoonery pay off. He had a strong sense of what he owed his constituents, and when elected he worked.

His lasting ignorance has been wrongly emphasized, even in works with pretensions to authority. Granted he only attended schools for a part of a year when he was nearly grown, but he didn't rest on his laurels, as most graduates of universities do. He was, for instance, in his middle thirties when he was sent to the state legislature. At first, as he later frankly confessed, he was in so much over his head that he simply didn't know what his colleagues were talking about. Neither dismayed by, nor truculent over, his deficiencies, he bided his time while he equipped himself to take part in debate.

Another man might have made the mistake of taking self-improvement so seriously as to make himself stiltedly inept. Crockett learned what he needed to without letting it starch the suppleness of his vernacular. By the time he reached Washington in 1828 he was ready for more advanced lessons in politics. He was also ready to give a few lessons himself.

Even the frontier had usually been represented by lawyers or by others with some pretensions to education and culture. Jackson, first of the frontier presidents, was not to bring his wild men across the mountains for another year. Crockett was a revelation to the East. He wore his coonskin cap on Pennsylvania Avenue. He told bear hunting stories in the fashionable taverns. He used the imaginative language of the border on the floor of the capitol. People laughed and called him an uncouth barbarian, but he won and held attention. When he addressed the House, the members from the older states were made conscious that a whole new and unknown section of the nation was speaking.

He was by no means a statesman, nor even a great politician, yet he had some of the best prerequisites. He was honest, was possessed of common sense, had an appreciation of men and was independent. Unfortunately these qualities are seldom valued in an opponent.

More than any president the United States has had, President Jackson was a political dictator. Moreover, he was from Crockett's home state and was known to have a death grip on the patronage there. A representative from Tennessee might then reasonably be expected to lease permanent space in the President's camp, and that's where most of them were found. Crockett, however, was nobody's hired man. He challenged Jackson's administration on one of the most important issues of the day—the question of what to do about the Indians east of the Mississippi.

Many charges have been leveled against Jackson in this connection, usually based on sentimentality rather than on a knowledge of what was going on. The real issue was not whether certain tribes could hold certain lands but whether they could live within the boundaries of sovereign states and account themselves an independent nation answerable to no authority wielded by either the state or the federal government. Once the principle was admitted and the precedent accepted the dangers were infinite. All the tribes that still had descendants in America could set themselves up as sovereign foreign countries, and white men, seeking protection for illicit enterprises, need only organize such nations to gain immunity from interference. Then, if the privilege was accorded Indians, why should it be denied to communities of whites who felt indisposed to obey laws or pay taxes?

Still many people couldn't see it, Crockett among them. He thought the government was morally bound to let the Cherokees, Choctaws and so on stay put, whether they insisted on sovereignty or not. It is a matter of record, too, that the Supreme Court of the day decided against the administration in what was supposed to be the test case to settle the point. The President was to ignore the adverse decision, but he did not ignore Crockett. He signaled to the Tennessee political machine, and Davy lost the next election.

As far as Crockett's character is concerned, the significant thing is that he struck out for what he conceived to be justice, even though championing Indians could not have been popular with the general run of his backwoods constituents. He had not entirely lost favor with them, however, and two years later he was back in Washington for a return engagement with the Jackson regime.

It was at this time that his reputation began climbing to unique heights from which it has never since descended. Crockettisms, real and invented, had been enlivening newspapers for some while. Now he emerged as the central figure of a literary fad that lasted for twenty odd years.

The first big gun fired was *Sketches and Eccentricities of Col. David Crockett of Tennessee,* a semi-fictitious work which the anonymous author coolly claimed to be authentic biography. Yet had the writer known what he was accomplishing, he would have been more anxious to father the book than to palm it off as fact. The Crockett fad aside, it was the initial volume of a remarkable literature destined to flourish for fifty years and whose like for a racy use of native material is unmatched in American or English letters.

That honor has often been accorded another book, but this, though without pretensions to Longstreet's pithy excellence, antedates *Georgia Scenes* by two years.

The literature referred to is the wonderful literature of the South, which most histories of American writing are careful to point out as nonexistent. It is now, unfortunately, all out of print; whereas in 1833 only one volume had ever been in it. Of itself *Sketches and Eccentricities* is as tentative as most beginnings, chiefly interesting for what it led to. It is spotty and ill-constructed but still makes fair reading.

Crockett was no man to blush and turn away from a spotlight, no matter how unexpected. He followed up *Sketches and Eccentricities* with *A Narrative of the Life of David Crockett written by Himself.* Commentators have tried to rob him of the authorship, claiming that it was either ghost written or the product of collaboration, but these are later cries, not heard in his day. His letters are ample proof that he was capable of putting coherent words on paper, and naturally he knew his subject. There appears to be no reason why the creation should be considered beyond his scope.

It is no great shakes as literature, but here and there an interesting personality shows through the amateur handling. But no matter what the handling, *Sketches* and *A Narrative* were something new in reading matter and people were quick to take notice. Editions soon appeared in England, creating a demand for more of the same on both sides of the Atlantic.

What had happened was that the American border had at last become articulate, and no one who heard could fail to note that something different had leaped whooping into literature. Previous American writing where it did not deliberately imitate that of Europe was demonstrably of the same seed. This of the frontier was indifferent to antecedents and unwatered by influences. If *Sketches and Eccentricities* was fraudulent, it yet held some of the wild flavor of border life. A *Narrative of the Life of David Crockett* established the genre, and others took it from there.

Davy's own further writings are problematical, although there are several candidates for consideration. His name is borne by two volumes appearing before his death, *An Account of Col. Crockett's Tour to the North and Down East* and *The Life of Martin Van Buren written by David Crockett.* In both his point of view, real or supposed, is brought to bear on rather unsuitable subjects. Some bibliographers also ascribe to him a curious work of fiction called *The Life and Adventures of Paddy O'Flarrity.* Though the title page makes an obvious attempt to hitch the work to Crockett's star, it can't be accepted as belonging. Davy wasn't the anonymous sort, and it seems probable that he would have done a better job.

Of far more importance to this chronicle than any of the others is a work entitled *Col. Crockett's Exploits and Adventures in Texas,* purportedly autobiographical and carrying him, indeed, up to the last day but one of the siege of the Alamo. It is a highly Borrovian work, antedating by some years the narratives of George Borrow. The latter may well have read and been influenced by this book, as the Crockett tales had an extensive English vogue, but that is not a point at issue here. What is important is the question as to how much fiction it contains. Estimates run from 100 per cent to a general acceptance of the narrative as fact.

The self-styled editor, now identified as the playwright, Richard Penn Smith, claimed that the narrative was taken verbatim from an actual journal kept by Crockett. Taken from him at the fall of the Alamo, it was found upon the person of a Mexican officer slain at the subsequent Battle of San Jacinto. A Texian officer, recognizing its worth, sent it to the States with the suggestion that it should be published. With the addition of only a preamble and an epilogue this was done. So much for the anonymous editor's story. Scholarship, originally skeptical, now leans toward giving it credence, at least to the extent of conceding that a Crockett diary supplied a factual basis for the book. The nature of the facts will come up for discussion further on.

Whether Davy had a hand in *Col. Crockett's Exploits and Adventures in Texas* or not, the tales of his prowess did not cease with his death. Moreover, he stepped out of regional literature and became general property. Before his demise he had won his way into that curious branch of American writing, the almanacs. As forerunners of the popular magazine, these booklets, officially dedicated to providing a predominantly rural people with meteorological data, had long been brightening their pages with stories, anecdotes and ballads. In the South especially the tall tales of the bear hunters had been favorite copy for this medium. Crockett had had his place, at first only as one among his peers, but by 1835 he started to dominate the field.

Crockett Almanacs originally appeared in Nashville, but the fad rapidly spread east and north. Soon Baltimore, Philadelphia, New York and Boston were turning them out annually. The hacks of the entire country pounced happily on this limitless subject and between them evolved a buckskin deity.

Crockett emerged as a titan capable of creating and righting cosmic disturbances. An alter ego was created for him in the person of Ben Hardin, the landlocked sailor. He had a pet bear called Deathhug and a team of alligators he hitched up when he wanted to ride the river to New Orleans. He was matched against Mike Fink. He engaged in mighty wrestlings and courted girls as formidable as Brynhild. As for his death in the Alamo, there was a school of thought which scoffed at the very possibility of Crockett's dying. He continued to have new adventures and to help in moving the frontier westward.

Yet at the time Crockett was commencing to be the delight of the nation he was going down to final political defeat. Returned to Washington in 1833, he arrived primed to do battle again with the administration of Andrew Jackson, who was not an almanac fan.

Crockett favored the use of Federal funds for internal improvements, something to which Old Hickory was strongly opposed. The former believed that public lands should be at the disposal of squatters; the latter did not. As bitterly as anything Crockett denounced Jackson's feud with the United States Bank. A quotation from one of his letters, written in 1834, will serve to show his feelings on the subject. It will also give some idea of why he was resented by the President:

You see our whole circulating medium deranged, and our whole commercial community destroyed, all to gratify the ambition of King Andrew the first, because the United States Bank refused to lend its aid in upholding his corrupt party; the truth is he is surrounded by a set of Imps of famin, that is willing to destroy the best interest of the country, to promote their own interest.

One point where Crockett and Jackson found themselves in agreement, however, was the question of annexing Texas. This could not be an open congressional issue, in as much as the United States was still at peace with Mexico, but it was an open issue as far as the public was concerned. Lobbies assailed the administration pro and con, and journalists discussed the matter with acrimonious freedom.

Most Americans still believed that Texas was properly a

part of the United States by virtue of Napoleon's sale. Furthermore, most Americans favored a policy of westward expansion that would give the country uncontested control of two balanced coast lines and the territory between them. At that point, however, approximate unanimity made way for sectionalism. The industrial power of the North was at odds with the agricultural South—principally over the matter of high protective tariffs, which were to the advantage of the former but were bankrupting the latter. Economically as well as geographically an annexed Texas would be of the South, and the North didn't want any more opposing votes in Congress. The South, already outvoted, wanted these new votes badly.

Jackson himself wanted Texas, but for once he could not assemble enough strength to be able to challenge the opposition. It is quite generally believed that Houston originally went to Texas as Jackson's agent, to work for independence by way of bringing about annexation. If that is true it is as far as Old Hickory got. Texas was at that time unofficially but firmly rejected by the United States because it was not of the same latitude as North Dakota or Nebraska.

There was the usual parade of virtue to justify the stand. Fronting for the North were its abolitionists, who had a field day. The Texians, by their account, were acting with the considered villainy to be expected of slave owners. Admitted to Mexico by a generous government operated by a crew of Nature's noblemen, the Texians had rewarded kindness with viciousness, a parent's loving care with bestial ingratitude. The gutters of Northern cities were flushed with tears for the injustice being done to that pinnacle of benevolence, Santa Anna.

In the South feeling was equally strong. Blood ties bound them to the colonists, strengthening the passion engendered

by partisanship and political necessity. There the Texians
were regarded as heroes to a man, and their cause was held
to be a holy one. Furthermore, a surprisingly large number of
the people weren't just talking. They dug into their socks for
money, they dispatched weapons, and they came themselves.
Companies of volunteers were formed at the expense of cities
and counties. Other men just climbed into the saddle and
jogged west by themselves.

It so happened that Crockett once more came up for re-
election in the fall of 1835. The papers of the United States,
approving and disapproving, were filled with the exploits of
the Texians and speculations as to the probable outcome of
the revolt. Crockett was then forty-nine but still active and
ardent. He is quoted as swearing that if he wasn't permitted
to serve his own country any longer his constituents could
go to Hell and he would go to Texas.

He was not re-elected. Once again President Jackson had
seen to it personally that he wasn't. When the congressional
term was over, therefore, Crockett set out to make good on
his oath. After first paying a visit to his family, he oiled up
Old Betsy, his rifle, and headed for the Mississippi.

The only detailed account of his trip is contained in *Col.
Crockett's Exploits and Adventures in Texas*, which may be
wholly apocryphal. Yet if fiction, it is fiction of a rare sort,
and it is a pity Richard Penn Smith didn't give up adapting
French plays and use a great deal more of his talents on that
branch of literature. Thimblerig, the Bee Hunter, the Pirate
and the Indian—whom Crockett picked up one by one in the
course of his fatal pilgrimage to the Alamo—are concepts
worthy to trot through the pages of *The Bible in Spain* and
Lavengro. It is with these four characters, following inci-
dents which scatter and reunite them, that he arrived in
Bexar.

This part of the narrative would appear to get some support from the memoirs of one J. M. Swisher, which include a circumstantial account of Crockett's sojourn at his father's house. Davy was then accompanied, Swisher stated, by only one man, a young chap. This could conceivably have been the Bee Hunter, with whom Crockett associated more than he did with any of the others.

Unfortunately for the acceptance of so winning a story as that of the five comrades, however, it does not jibe with the recollection of Dr. Sutherland, who stated that Crockett joined the garrison with a train of twelve Tennesseans. In this he is supported by the records of the provisional government which indicate that Crockett was commander of a "company" of Tennessee Mounted Volunteers. Presumably but not provedly the twelve accompanied him all the way from his native state.

Yet the *Exploits and Adventures* fall in line with history when Crockett is made to describe the informal attitude of the garrison. His cordial meetings with Travis and Bowie are also recounted, if not accurately at least in a manner that carries conviction. And, of course, he took an interest in the famous knife.

Of the weapon he remarked: "I wish I may be shot if it wasn't enough to give a man of squeamish stomach the colic, especially before breakfast." Noting his interest, Bowie commented: "Colonel, you might tickle a fellow's ribs a long time with this little instrument without making him laugh; and many a time have I seen a man puke at the idea of the point touching the pit of his stomach."

Dr. Sutherland furnished a more businesslike report of his actions upon arrival. Crockett refused a command of relative importance, which Travis pressed upon him. Although a militia colonel, he said that all he wanted was to be regarded "as a sort of high private." By this he meant to indicate, it can be assumed, that he didn't want to be bothered either by taking orders or by giving them to anybody but his Tennesseans.

The garrison members, who had been much cheered when Bowie arrived, were greatly gratified at the presence of the other—Mike Fink having died some years before—chief legendary figure of the old Southwest. To satisfy the popular demand Crockett made a speech complete with some of his famous anecdotes. By Sutherland's account it went over big, and at its conclusion Davy was among friends.

This was hardly to be wondered at, for in the Alamo he was among his own kind. Though *sui generis* in quite a few respects, he was a standard forest product in so many others. He had a natural kinship with the majority of the defenders of the fortress, which could not be claimed by such a typical frontiersmen as Bowie and Travis.

Most of them, like him, had spent most of their lives as hunters, trappers and small-clearing farmers. They had lived, just as he had, largely in cabins of their own building. Their feet, too, had spent more time in moccasins than they had in shoes. Most of them likewise had got their education, if any, on their own initiative. They didn't have to see Crockett's coonskin cap to know his background. When he talked they could smell the bear blood and wood smoke.

As he had arrived on February 11, old home week stretched into twelve days. At the end of that period the stir among the Mexican population gave the Texians the first warning they were willing to heed, and Sutherland went on his historic scouting mission.

When the doctor returned to report to Travis he found Crockett in the latter's company. Davy then asked what part of the fort he and his Tennesseans should defend and was assigned to what, as shall be seen, was probably the most vulnerable section of the walls. There can be no doubt that Travis was aware of it, and the obvious conclusion is that he gave Crockett the spot as a post of honor. At all events it was accepted unhesitatingly.

The troops which Sutherland and Smith had seen were some squadrons of cavalry, not prepared of themselves to attack a fortress. Several hours intervened before their infantry and artillery support caught up with them, and it was not until then—about 2:00 P.M.—that the first section of the Mexican army occupied Bexar. Meanwhile Sutherland and Smith were off on a new mission.

When the doctor had dismounted to report, the leg injured when his horse fell buckled under him. Examining himself a few minutes later he found that he had a knee injury which seemed likely to cripple him for weeks. Seeing that he was unfit for his normal duties, Bowie and Travis decided that he would be most useful in the capacity of courier. A messenger or two having already been ordered to Goliad to ask Colonel Fannin for assistance, Sutherland was sent to Gonzales; and as soon as he had rested his leg somewhat he left. He had gone but a little way when he met Smith, also entrusted with an appeal for aid.

Climbing the low hills on the east side of the San Antonio River Valley between three and four o'clock on the twenty-third of February, 1836, they heard a cannon shot and turned to look back. The Military Plaza, beside which the old Presidio of San Antonio de Bexar had once stood, was filled with Mexican soldiers. The shot had come from the Alamo's heaviest piece, an eighteen-pounder, and it was promptly answered by a Mexican gun. Batteries had already been drawn up on the west bank of the river.

Sutherland and Smith pushed on, unaware until later that

they had not witnessed the beginning of hostilities. Following the two shots they had heard there was a brief parley. The Mexicans asked for it by raising a white flag, and two officers from the Alamo were sent to learn what the enemy had to say. These two found themselves addressed by Colonel Juan Almonte, speaking for Santa Anna, who didn't reach Bexar until several hours later. The Colonel demanded unconditional surrender, to which Bowie and Travis replied that they weren't going to capitulate, with conditions or without.

From that moment the siege was officially on, and Mexicans showed themselves within rifle range at their peril. It took them a while to learn just what effective rifle range meant to an American frontiersman. Just after the brief truce a Mexican walked into the clear at what he conceived to be a safe distance and was promptly picked off. Tradition has it —and in the case of the man involved tradition is as acceptable as assured fact—that the firer of this shot, for the first blood of the engagement, was Davy Crockett.

VIII

SANTA ANNA

WHEN Santa Anna crossed the Rio Grande in February, 1836, it was not the first time he had marched to put down rebellion in Texas. Almost a quarter of a century before he had been with Arredondo.

The occasion had been the revolt promoted by Magee and Guttierez in 1812. It was then that the flag of Texas as an independent state had first been raised and, as in the fall of 1835, the Mexican garrisons had all been conquered. The North American filibusters had been just about convinced that their revolution was successful when Arredondo trapped them and cut them to pieces.

Santa Anna had been with Arredondo when he hunted the fugitives down with lancers, and when he had entered Bexar. He had been with him when he had taken the Alamo and murdered part of the surrendered garrison as an object lesson. Then Santa Anna had been only eighteen, but he was a veteran of two years' standing who had earned his commission in the field. Now he was President of Mexico, and much more than that. He was Mexico's most capable and most interesting, if by no means her worthiest, citizen.

Antonio Lopez de Santa Anna Perez de Lebron was born in 1794 in Jalapa, which hangs several thousand feet above Mexico's great port of Vera Cruz. His father was a *gachupine,* which is to say a Spaniard born, while his mother was a creole, or a Mexican claiming pure Spanish blood. The family seems to have been comfortably situated but no more than that.

The son grew to be a lithe, active man of five feet ten. His portraits show lively eyes set in a sallow, melancholy face. It has been pointed out that he looked more like a scholarly professional man than the adventurer he was.

It would be useless to hazard estimates of his motives from point to point in the account of his activities which follows, so commentary will be put in capsule form here. He was a consummate gambler. He was whatever he wanted to be, capable of magnanimity even—if it served his purpose. As the nature of villainy can be no more than a wreaking of one's own will in despite of all principle, he was one of history's complete villains. Beyond that he had no character: he just did things. In contrast to his three chief antagonists at the Alamo he survived, though the rest of his incredible career has no place in this chronicle.

To begin: Like Sam Houston, whom he was later to meet, Santa Anna was scheduled for a commercial career by his family, and, like Houston, Santa Anna absolutely refused. The American avoided it, after a brief trial, by going off to live with the Cherokees. The Mexican succeeded in getting his father to sign him up as a cadet in a regiment stationed at Vera Cruz. That was in 1810, when he was only sixteen years old. Spanish rule was still taken for granted, especially by the army, and the youngster had no thought beyond attaining distinction as an officer of Spain.

The year 1810, however, marked the first popular revolt

against Spain; and there had been forerunners in the struggles for power among upper-class groups. To understand not only Santa Anna but the whole confused course of Mexican history where it bears on the Texas Revolution it is necessary to take a brief look at what was then happening and why.

Mexico charged Spain with many grievances, but the insults to pride and the pocketbook were the ones most taken to heart. No native-born Mexican, no matter what his education, ancestry, or wealth, was permitted to hold a government position of any importance. The *gachupine* office holders thus formed a ruling class which looked down upon the creoles. The theory supposedly behind this law was that nobody born outside the superior atmosphere of Spain was fit to govern. Actually it had a much more practical basis. By establishing a class division between the Spanish and the native-born, the rulers were kept mindful of the fact that their interests were exclusively bound up with the mother country. The second great grievance was assisted by the first. Mexico annually dumped millions of pesos into the bottomless coffers of Spain, but Spain sent Mexico very little in return except more officials to see that the money kept coming.

In the close to three hundred years that this had been going on even a people conditioned to autocracy could eventually work up resentment. The chance for an outlet to bad feeling was first offered by the Napoleonic wars. Among the things Bonaparte requisitioned was the throne of Spain, which he handed to his brother. The ties of loyalty the creoles had always felt they owed to the Spanish royal family were no longer operative, and the native-born began to feel their oats.

One Spanish group declared outright that Mexico might belong to a Spanish king but could not to a French one and that therefore the sovereignty had reverted to the people of the country. They so worked on the viceroy, no Bonapartist himself, that he agreed to convoke a national congress; but some other *gachupines* feared the result might be that the creoles would get a cut of the political pie and deposed the viceroy. They were able then to suppress the first move by the creoles for separation from Spain in 1809.

The idea had become contagious, however. Hitherto there had been only three powerful groups, the *gachupines*, the creoles and the clergy; but a priest called Father Miguel Hidalgo raised a new standard of revolt. In part it was aimed at the independence of Mexico, but its broader issues were more important as far as the majority of the people were concerned. Influenced by the French Revolution, Father Hidalgo went to war for the extension of ordinary civil rights to the mestizos and Indians. That was in 1810, the year of Santa Anna's military apprenticeship.

Hidalgo's revolt was soon put down, but from then on rebellion, often indistinguishable from banditry, was a commonplace of Mexican history. It was particularly hard to stamp out in the north, far from the capital, and General Joaquin de Arredondo was sent to put it down wherever found. Among Arredondo's troops was the regiment from Vera Cruz. As this was early in 1811 young Santa Anna had had only a few months of barracks life before, at the age of seventeen, he saw action.

He turned out to be a natural campaigner, with a love for life in the field and the smell of gunpowder that he never outlived. Arredondo was a skillful raider, skirmisher and Indian fighter who followed up victory with brutality, and who rewarded his soldiery by turning captured cities over to them. That was how he acted when he took Bexar on Santa Anna's first visit to the town.

In spite of the fact that he'd forged his general's name to help himself over a bad spot in a gambling game, Santa Anna got along well on this campaign, which lasted nearly three years. He had eased through the court martial on the strength of a good field record, and he returned to Vera Cruz a first lieutenant, decorated for bravery under fire.

His experience in the north was excellent training for his next assignment, which was that of keeping the roads around Vera Cruz free of the infinity of bandits who thronged thereabouts. Always conducting himself with vigor and boldness, he had won himself a captaincy and two more decorations by the time he was twenty-seven. He had then been in the army eleven years and had spent over ten of them in the most active kind of service.

That year of 1821 was the year Mexico finally achieved independence, and up to that time he had given no evidence of having a political thought in his head. As a member of His Most Catholic Majesty's Army he was against rebels, and apparently he let it go at that. For the rest he indulged in the usual off-duty pursuits of gambling, drinking and love-making, but never so much as to interfere with his work. In a word he led an uncomplicated existence in a monstrously mixed up society.

In the course of its development Mexico had evolved, among other things, a caste system second only to that of India in depth and complexity. Born in Olympus itself were the *gachupines*, but even these were graded. Everybody who comes to a new country can reasonably claim to have been a prince in the old one. However, all, which was of importance here, couldn't produce Castilian accents. The *gachupines*, then, were sorted according to the political standing of the Spanish provinces from which they came. Yet no matter where they hailed from, their birthplace assured them enfranchisement and power.

Next in order came the bona fide creoles, ranked according to the native provinces of their ancestry. Below them were those whom nobody could exactly prove not to be pure creoles, and beneath them again were creoles by courtesy— the ones who looked white enough to get by in a country where the whites were so outnumbered they were looking for recruits. With the blood, pure or assumed, went social standing and privilege but not enfranchisement.

Far lower down were the mestizos, the half-breeds whose Indian blood was so obvious it could not be ignored. But a mestizo by a *gachupine* father outranked one engendered by a creole. They were also divided into half, quarter, eighth and sixteenth breeds. At this point standing and privilege ceased, but serfdom might be escaped.

Lower again were the mulattoes, graded by color; the Indians who formed the majority of the population; and the mixed Indian and Negro. Except for the Indians who hadn't been reduced, these belonged to anybody who could hold on to them. They couldn't legally be sold, but that was the only article on their bill of rights. Last of all were the Negro slaves. Due to the serfs, however, these were not numerous.

In a way the caste system was better designed to abet wretchedness and discontent than that of India, for even those at the very top could not have found it wholly pleasing. The *gachupine* could not perpetuate his own lordly kind but begat disfranchised creole children.

Yet though all these rigidities dominated social life in Mexico, generally speaking, that life was also in a state of flux. The Spanish experiment of adapting instead of exterminating or moving the native population had reached a stage that might have been anticipated but probably was not. As the

country developed and the cities grew without a correspond-
ing growth in the white population, property ownership and
its perquisites began to come into the hands of some of the
mestizos. Their struggle for an even fuller recognition—and
this would break the ice to render society a fluid in which
even the Indian could swim—was just beginning to be felt, so
nobody could really feel secure.

In that welter of discontent the only professions which
offered any measure of security were those of the churchman
and the soldier. Yet in 1820 even the church and the army
got a shaking from Spain. Liberals temporarily in power
there took away some of the special privileges which had
made military and clerical life desirable. The general effect
was to deprive Spanish rule in Mexico of its two most powerful props. The specific effect was that for the first time the
forces of rebellion could find trained officers to lead them.

An officer called Agustin Iturbide soon took the leadership
of the entire rebellion out of the hands of the liberals who
had started it. The latter were dreaming of a revolution on
the all-pervasive lines of the French one Napoleon had
stultified, and Iturbide let them promise the people an end
of caste and special privilege. A democracy was the last
thing he had on his mind, though. He and his military supporters wanted Mexican independence, but they couldn't
conceive of national sovereignty without a national sovereign. Their concept, as stated in the "Plan of Iguala," which
Iturbide published in February, 1821, was of an independent
Mexico ruled by a prince selected from the Spanish royal
family.

Santa Anna at first stood with the Royalist party, but after
defeating the rebels in one engagement he suddenly changed
sides in the midst of a battle. As the Royalists had just promoted him to hold him and as the insurgent forces had to

promote him to win him over, he emerged from this change of heart with a colonelcy.

Once he had joined the rebels, Santa Anna turned on his former comrades without pausing for breath and soon was in control of his district. This included Vera Cruz, which was not only the country's largest port but was one which Spain had succeeded in holding after her troops had been driven from most other strongholds. On his first attack Santa Anna took a beating, but after a land blockade lasting several months he entered the city, leaving only the island citadel which guarded the port in hostile hands.

Meanwhile Iturbide had persuaded the Spanish viceroy to agree to the Plan of Iguala. Spain repudiated the treaty, neither abandoning the forts she still occupied nor sending over a prince; but victory remained with the Mexicans, and they celebrated accordingly. All that they had to do now was to form themselves into a nation.

It should be borne in mind that here was a people who had been denied all right to rule themselves beyond organizing town councils. Furthermore the only popular plan for a government had been knocked on the head when Spain refused to supply a ruler. For the first difficulty there was no cure but time. Iturbide had a way to get around the other, though. He offered himself. The republicans had succeeded in getting a majority in the congress of delegates convoked to decide upon the matter, but a majority wasn't enough. A minority elected Iturbide emperor when the rest weren't looking, and he was crowned Agustin I in 1822.

Santa Anna's good work during the revolution admitted him to the inner circle of the imperial court. He tried to crowd even closer by courting the emperor's elderly sister, but Iturbide gave him the brush off. Nevertheless, the latter promoted him to brigadier and made his position as military commander of Vera Cruz official.

There's more than a suggestion that the promotion was due to a growing conviction on the Emperor's part that here was a tiger in need of placating. As always in such cases it was not enough. Santa Anna's correspondence with Agustin I was warmed with vows of adoration strong enough to make deity blush; but the Emperor knew him—and by then the new Brigadier was beginning to know himself.

Somewhere in the year that he had been associated with the intrigues with which rebellions can seldom dispense, he had learned more than courtly phrases. He had discovered there were far swifter ways of getting promotion than attending to duty. He had been given power, political as well as military, and found he had a taste for it. He had also discovered that boldness, bluff and a shrewd ruthlessness would serve him as well in political maneuvers as they did in the field.

Iturbide already had a great many things to worry him besides the Brigadier. It took only a few months for Mexicans to find out that being citizens of an independent country wasn't of itself paradise. About the same time they discovered that Agustin I was working harder at acting as he thought an emperor should than he was at trying to construct the nation. To do him justice, it was a task which only supreme greatness could have tackled with any hope of success, but he didn't even know how to begin. Nobody but his court favorites were satisfied, and public irritation was taking voice.

Some claim that the Emperor's rebuff in regard to his sister had alienated Santa Anna, but the probabilities seem to favor a course of action based more on opportunism than pique. At any rate, the Brigadier abruptly stopped playing kiss-your-hand with Agustin I. It was not so much that he held very many high cards himself, but that at a meeting between the two he saw that Iturbide—who had become emperor by the exercise of pure brass—was beginning to lose his nerve. Acting with the intuitive boldness of the successful conspirator, Santa Anna publicly announced that the empire must give way to a republic.

This marked the first time he had been anything but a follower. Likewise it marked the first time he had been known to give democracy a thought. However, the congress which Iturbide had hornswoggled into letting him have an imperial crown was known to have been strongly republican. Santa Anna's move was as logical as it was dangerous.

At the time he was no more than a provincial commandant. He not only didn't have a following, but in Vera Cruz, where he published his announcement, he was extremely unpopular. He did not even have a specific policy which would serve to rally men to him. Yet once he was out on the limb he showed skill at balancing. Only twenty-eight, he could have been pardoned for thrusting himself too far forward, but he knew better. Instead he chose Guadalupe Victoria, an old-time Republican who had refused to recognize Iturbide's regime, to be the political head of the movement.

The revolt instantly drew a large national following, but at first it didn't appear to be large enough. Santa Anna lost the first major engagement with imperial troops and thought of leaving the country. The tide turned just in time to see his gamble through, however. Agustin I had been crowned in May, 1822 and by March, 1823 he was finished.

The Plan of Iguala had been succeeded by the Plan of Casa Mata, which was actually no plan at all. Its sole specific affirmation was that the government should be reorganized, leaving the direction of reorganization up in the air. A commission of three generals was appointed by the successful rebels to govern while congress weighed the matter, but Santa Anna wasn't one of them. As yet neither his military nor his political reputation could match those of several other people. Reluctant to be overshadowed, he left the capital and went off campaigning in the north.

The rebels having succeeded, those against them were now rebels. Some of these were in action in northern Mexico, but Santa Anna did little to bother them. On the other hand he bothered the citizens of San Luis Potosi, where he quartered his troops, a great deal. Having failed to build up political strength, another man might have pulled in his horns. Santa Anna replied to local criticism by staging a military demonstration at which he publicly declared himself to be in favor of the federal form of republican government.

Luck and foresight are often hard to distinguish, but Santa Anna bet on the right long-shot horse so many times he must be given credit for an unusual knowledge of form. Mexico still possessed strong Royalist and Iturbidist factions. Although leaning toward democracy, the constitutional convention then meeting was known to be divided as to the kind of democracy to be adopted.

As in the case of his statement calling for a rebellion against the Emperor, the action nearly cost Santa Anna his position if not his life. His own troops were divided on the political issue involved and went to war with each other on the spot. Hearing of the disturbance, the interim government sent a force to take over San Luis Potosi. Santa Anna withdrew but finally gave himself up and submitted to court martial.

Just as he was in the pot, with the fire laid under him, however, the constitutional convention did decide upon a federal republic. Furthermore, a special session of the convention had been called to consider Santa Anna's proclamation not long before the form of government decided upon was announced. The case against him was quietly dropped, and the new administration soon gave him the most important post he had yet held.

The constitution which he had thus helped to promote was that of 1824. In a general way it was modeled on that of the United States of America. It called for a federation of sovereign states to be ruled by an elective president and a bicameral congress.

The provision which had the greatest effect on the history of the Alamo was the one specifying that a region having less than eighty thousand inhabitants could not aspire to statehood. It was a reasonable stipulation, aimed neither at Texas nor at North Americans, for as yet immigration had barely commenced.

It was not until October, 1824 that the constitution was finally adopted. Long before that Santa Anna had been called from temporary retirement and made military governor of Yucatan. Taking his bride, the former Dona Ines Garcia, he arrived there in May, destined to spend about a year.

Western Yucatan, trading with other parts of Mexico, was sympathetic to the republic. Eastern Yucatan depended on Spanish trade and wanted either to belong to Spain or to be an independent nation. Havana was much nearer the district than Mexico City, so the Spanish faction was strengthened by the active support of representatives of Mexico's mother country, still not resigned to losing so vast a territory. Obeying his orders to hold Yucatan at all costs, Santa Anna shortly found himself the civil as well as military power in the region. Yucatan was held and peace was established between

the two warring sections of the state, but Santa Anna himself was again in trouble.

Not content with holding off Spain, he decided to carry
the war to her by capturing Havana; and he actually assembled a large flotilla for that amphibious operation. Whether
he knew it or not, he was by that gesture stepping into big
league international politics. Havana controlled the northern
and western approaches to the Caribbean, a sea in which the
United States, France and England shared Spain's interest.
Nobody could upset the *status quo* there without being challenged by all of them. Pressure was brought to bear and, to
his intense disgust, Santa Anna was recalled.

There was also a demand that he be court martialed, but
that was old hat as far as he was concerned. Besides he had
not acted without official knowledge, if not blessing. The
Secretary of War, Gomez Pedraza, was known to have remarked that Mexico would benefit whether Santa Anna succeeded in taking Havana or got his head chopped off trying.
Then, as it happened, the first president of Mexico was
Guadalupe Victoria, who owed his position to Santa Anna in
no small degree. He merely explained the situation to his
general and let the court martial stand in place of a repri-
mand. It was a gentle substitute, for though the charges
weren't dropped, neither were they prosecuted.

For two years afterward Santa Anna played the country
squire on his estates near his home town of Jalapa. It wasn't
until there was a split in the nation promoted by a Masonic
feud that he again became a public figure. The Scottish Rite
Masons were pro-Spanish and in favor of a centralized form
of republican government as opposed to the federal form.
The York Ritists, in favor of the liberal federal form, were
newly organized. They had, in fact, been sponsored by J. R.

Poinsett, a United States diplomatic agent who believed in fighting fire with fire. These branches of the brotherhood were so strong that they just about divided the man power of the country.

The Yorkists being in control, it was up to the Scottish Ritists to try to come up from below. When they did make the attempt they were headed by no less a person than Nicholas Bravo, the nation's Vice-President.

Santa Anna first played along with the Scottish Rite Masons, but when the big explosion came he swiftly turned Yorkist. The projected rebellion had its chief support in Vera Cruz where, because of the town's dependence on Spanish trade, Spanish influence was particularly strong. When Santa Anna, upon whom the rebels had strongly counted, offered his services to the government the opposition wilted forthwith. The incident served not only to show how influential he had become, but it gave a last-minute save to his reputation as a liberal.

Having put the Scottish Rite branch in its place, the Yorkist tribe of the Masonic fellowship staged an intramural fight. The split was in part racial, as the two presidential candidates for the election of 1828 were the creole, Gomez Pedraza, and the mestizo, Vicente Guerrero. Pedraza received most of the votes found in the ballot boxes, but that wasn't allowed to settle the issue. For one thing there was talk of skulduggery; for another, President-Elect Pedraza began prematurely using his prestige for the oppression of his political enemies.

Listed number one among them was Santa Anna. The feud had begun when Pedraza, as Secretary of War, had insulted the General on several occasions. The General was a creole, but in the election he cast his vote for the Secretary's mestizo opponent and tried to get everybody else to do so. Once

elected, Pedraza retaliated by preferring charges and ar-
ranging a court martial manned by officers who hated Santa
Anna.

Knowing he would be shot if caught, the latter gathered
a band of men and seized the strong fortress of Perote, some
forty miles from Jalapa. For this he was declared an outlaw,
and strong forces of government troops converged upon him.
After sustaining a brief siege he had to abandon Perote because of lack of supplies and fought a rear-guard action all
the two hundred miles to Oaxaca. Holed up in that city, he
was in desperate straits when the situation suddenly turned
in his favor.

He owed this break in fortune not to luck but to his own
positive action. At the time he had captured Perote he had
declared that he was in the field not for himself but for the
defeated candidate, Vicente Guerrero. Pedraza, his manifesto
stated, was an enemy of federal republicanism and must go.
The movement thus started swiftly became a national one,
culminating in Pedraza's exile just in time to save its origi-
nator's neck. Guerrero was declared President-Elect and
made Secretary of War while he waited to take office. In this
capacity he showed his gratitude by promoting Santa Anna
from brigadier to general of division; and as soon as he
became President he made the General governor of the state
of Vera Cruz. The decree of outlawry hadn't yet been withdrawn, but that didn't matter.

At about this time Spain once more threatened. She had
been watching the troubles in Mexico with great interest and
had concluded that conditions were now favorable for recap-
turing the country. The logical point of attack was Vera
Cruz, and the new governor vigorously started on his preparations for a defense. But logic wasn't followed, and at the
last minute Mexican agents sent a report that the Spanish

flotilla was headed for Tampico, 250 miles north of Vera Cruz.

That put it out of Santa Anna's jurisdiction, barring special orders, which he neither received nor waited for. He knew if he sent to Mexico City Spain would have a foothold before he got an answer. He therefore commandeered every ship in the port, put his troops aboard, and set sail.

It was one of those actions that would have been absolutely indefensible and unforgivable if it hadn't worked out. He had deserted his post and left Vera Cruz vulnerable. Except for his frustrated attempt against Havana he knew nothing whatever about amphibious operations. He had no naval support. His force numbered only about half the four thousand Spanish troops he was sailing to meet. For all this he has been much criticized. Yet if he had done the correct thing Spain might very well have succeeded in reconquering his country. Once she'd got a grip she would have received strong support from Mexican factions.

As it turned out the Spanish weren't quite as strong as had been reported, and they had picked a bad spot to land. The poisonous coast near Tampico was more lethal than the savage attack Santa Anna delivered in August, 1829. The combination was too much, though the invaders held out for two weeks of intermittent skirmishing and parleying before a second pitched battle forced capitulation.

A week after he had sailed, congress had authorized Santa Anna to employ his troops outside of Vera Cruz, so there was not even a technicality to mar his triumph when he returned to his proper post as the nation's liberator. He did not, however, immediately cash in on his victory. Nor did he accept the leadership of the rebel party that was shortly offered him.

Rebellion had long been a chronic condition in Mexico, but

recent events had tended to give the military challenge of election returns a sort of legal sanction. Guerrero had, with Santa Anna's prompting, snatched the presidency from Pedraza in the name of the popular will. Now the new Vice-President, Anastasio Bustamente, set out to do the people a similar favor by ousting Guerrero. Ostensibly he did it to promote the reinstatement of Pedraza, but in the upshot he took the chief executive's chair himself.

During this upheaval Santa Anna's conduct was correct, to anybody's taste. When he first heard Guerrero was in difficulties he marched to his support, but upon learning that the President had thrown in the sponge and fled, he returned quietly to Jalapa. Nor would he accept tempting offers from the Bustamente regime.

His whole history showed how reckless he could be when nothing else would serve; but a man who only understands that much of gambling will never be more than an amateur. A really accomplished gambler knows when to hew to the line—and when to do nothing. By making the proper gesture followed by a dignified withdrawal, Santa Anna grew in strength while the furiously active Bustamente steadily lost ground.

Not only Mexico but the rest of the world marked Santa Anna's course with approval. He became famous for the very qualities he least possessed. The agents of foreign governments wrote home that he was a man of rocklike integrity, unswervingly dedicated to republican principles. The Texians, upon whom the Bustamente regime was pressing hard, began to look upon him as the hero who might save them from oppression.

Santa Anna waited until the demand for him became a national clamor before he threw his hat in the ring, and when he did so it was not in his own name. To have started a revolution in his own name would have destroyed the character of a die-hard constitutionalist, which he had carefully established for himself. Yet he could make one move that was the essence of constitutionalism. He backed the reinstatement of Pedraza, the duly-elected candidate who had never been permitted to serve a day of his term.

It was Santa Anna himself—under sufficient provocation, it must be granted—who had been responsible for the shunting aside of Pedraza in the first place; but in three years everybody had forgotten about that. At the tag end of 1832 Pedraza got to be President for three months. The man who had once feared to have him in that position had so grown in power that he could use him as a pawn.

In the election of 1832 Santa Anna was not only the people's choice, but he got the most votes. The General knew all about Mexican elections by then, and he saw to it that no faction but his own was permitted to stuff the ballot boxes. In the interest of appearances his running mate was a simon-pure liberal named Gomez Farias.

Now the record becomes amazing. Having won the presidency by a marvelous mixture of fair means and foul, Santa Anna asked and received permission to turn his duties over to the Vice-President while he rested from the fatigues of campaigning. The truth was that while his vanity craved the power and reveled in the prestige connected with the office, the work attached to it bored him. He enjoyed fighting and maneuvering for the presidency; but once he'd won he preferred the sports and informal luxury of a wealthy landowner's life to the routine of governing. Leaving Mexico City, he retired to the immense estates he had somehow acquired.

Given a free hand, Farias began to justify all the hopes that the liberals had built on the foundation of Santa Anna's reputation. The Acting President knew what the country needed and feared nobody. In addition to sponsoring many beneficial measures he made headway toward breaking the strangleholds which the army and the clergy had on national affairs.

Unfortunately he was talking over the heads of his congress and of the rest of the country. It is the natural desire of a man of excellent ideas to wish to make use of power by putting them all into execution right away. The unsettling fact is that people won't be pressed toward reforms for which they are mentally unprepared. The basically illiterate Mexican population was geared to take its guidance from the church, whose interest lay in seeing that it remained basically illiterate. Farias got just so far with his enlightened program when popular feeling turned against him.

From his comfortable vantage point President Santa Anna was watching developments carefully. While Farias was being applauded, the General, as titular head of the administration, took full credit for an aggressive liberalism. When Farias began to lose ground Santa Anna made it clear that he had not been consulted when the reforms were promulgated. Once convinced that national feeling was strongly antagonistic to the Farias regime, he abandoned the liberal movement overnight and without apology.

There was now a contest that made it worth while for him to be in office again. He entered one side of Mexico City just as Acting-President Farias was hastening out the other. The man who was attempting to bring literacy and all the social benefits which go with it into the country was execrated as a monster. The church hailed Santa Anna as its savior. The populace hailed him with the relief of a boy being rescued from a bath.

The change had been so sudden that liberals at first

couldn't believe that their erstwhile leader was betraying them. They soon found out; and those who moved fast enough lived to spread the news. *Vae victis* and winner take all were Mexican political laws which Santa Anna honored. He had often put his own neck on the line while reaching for power, and he did not spare others now that he had it.

He was denounced as a renegade to liberalism, but there has to be faith before there can be apostasy. All that had happened was that he was nudged by his instinct for the course which would not only serve him for the moment but would lead to a strengthening of his position. It was usually infallible, and it did not let him down now.

As a federal Republican he had reached the permissible zenith of power when he became President. Changing to conservatism, however, opened a new field. It so happened that in Mexico the extreme conservatives were for a centralized form of government unbalanced by state sovereignty. The President under such a system would be twice the figure of one under a federal system with its well contrived checks against autocracy. That was something new to strive for, and Santa Anna went after it.

He worked slowly and carefully until in January, 1835 he was given a hand-picked congress recruited from the clergy and the army. After that it was too easy. Unwilling to be bothered with the details, he once more retired to Jalapa while somebody else put through his program. By October, 1835 state governorships were appointive, state legislatures were disbanded, and the constitution which held such a condition contrary to the law of the land had been scrapped in favor of one which approved. The transition from a federal to a centralized government was complete.

Santa Anna was not without occupation meanwhile. There was local dissatisfaction with his program, but serious rebellion was offered by only two sections of the nation. One was the State of Zacatecas, which refused to disband its state militia. Santa Anna himself led the force which defeated that militia, and he was in the state capital looking on while his soldiers indulged in unrestrained rapine until they were sated. The other part of Mexico where the people chose to fight for their rights was the old province of Texas.

Aware of the feeling on that distant frontier, Santa Anna had, since June of 1835, planned either to lead or send a force north of the Rio Grande which would overawe the obstreperous populace once and for all. Busy with other matters, for the time being, though, he had contented himself with strengthening the forces in the region. Then finally disturbed by reports of the activities of the War party, he ordered his brother-in-law, General Cos, to move from Matamoras to Bexar and sit on the lid until he, Santa Anna, got ready to do more than that.

The provisional government's declaration of war naturally speeded up his plans for overrunning Texas, but it was still a project for the late spring or thereabouts of the following year. It was the unexpected defeat of Cos in December, 1835 that made Santa Anna definitely decide to head the punitive force himself. His brother-in-law's defeat tarnished his own prestige, let alone the fact that Mexican regulars had been conquered by amateurs. Exerting the frenzied energy of which he alone was capable in Mexico, he prepared to attack in mid-winter.

The constant revolutions and counterrevolutions had whittled the army away until not too many regulars could be spared for an expeditionary force. The nation's credit had been badly damaged on the same rocks. In spite of these handicaps Santa Anna scraped together an army of eight thousand men and drove them on short rations through the winter-harried upland deserts of northern Mexico. Men and animals perished by the hundreds, but at the tail end of February, 1836 the troops were at the Rio Grande.

There the force was augmented by Cos and his men, released on parole. Of this vow never to fight against the Texians who had chivalrously freed them, Santa Anna made short work. He ordered his brother-in-law to quit talking nonsense and to fall his men in for the return trip to Bexar. Cos complied.

Also under El Presidente's orders was a brigade or so which had come to join him from Matamoras under the leadership of General Jose Urrea. While Santa Anna proceeded against Bexar, Urrea's orders were to advance on Goliad. El Presidente's scouting and espionage services were reliable, and he knew those to be the only two strongholds in Texas. Once they were taken, his columns would be in a position to chop up the colonies unopposed.

His plans for the inhabitants had already been itemized. All leaders and principal promoters of the revolution were to be executed. The cost of his expedition was to be defrayed by the seizure of property. All participators in the rebellion were to be exiled. All volunteers and transient adventurers who had entered the region since 1828 were to be treated as pirates. No Anglo-American would be allowed to remain west of the Sabine.

Santa Anna's men crossed the Rio Grande at Laredo, but did not go as a body, because of inadequate water and forage along the way. Columns of about fifteen hundred men apiece, each two or three days' journey behind the one in front, set forth in turn. Estimates of the total force which thus marched the last 150 miles to Bexar range from six to ten thousand, though the first figure is probably more nearly correct.

The President himself led the first column, although he did not arrive with the vanguard which had demanded the surrender of the Alamo. Well informed as to conditions in Bexar, he did not anticipate much in the way of opposition, but when he reached the old Texas capital in the course of the afternoon of February 23, the flag of rebellion still flew over the fortress.

Finding this to be the case, Santa Anna raised a flag of his own, though it was not the military ensign of his country. From the tower of San Fernando Cathedral, the highest point in Bexar, there alternately drooped and flew in the winds a blood-red banner in sign that no quarter would be given to the garrison of the Alamo.

Part III

THE SIEGE OF THE ALAMO

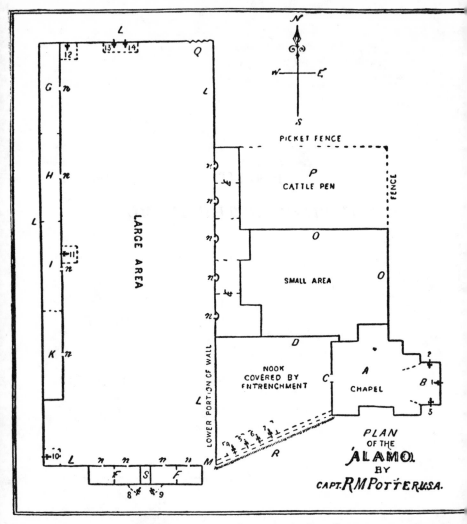

LEGEND: (A) *chapel*, (B) *apse*, (C) *doorway*, (D) *wall connecting chapel and* long barracks, (E) *long barracks*, (F) *south barracks*, (G, H, I & K) *separate* stone rooms, (L) *walls of old mission plaza*, (M) *main gateway*, (n) *doors to* barracks and stone rooms, (O) *low stone walls*, (P) *cattle pen*, (Q) *breach in* wall, (R) *entrenchment and earthwork*, (S) *porte-cochere, protected by lunette.* *The numbers 1–14 show the location of the fort's cannon.*

IX

THE FORT AND THE GARRISON

AT THE time the siege began, the Texians were still a week short of declaring for independence, creating a new republic, and hoisting the Lone Star flag which symbolized it. The flag Santa Anna saw above the Alamo was Mexican, differing from those borne by his troops in one respect only. Superimposed on the national colors of Mexico were the significant numerals, 1824. They stood for, of course, the old liberal constitution which Santa Anna himself had destroyed.

The stronghold beneath that standard of defiance fell a long ways short of fulfilling the recognized functions of a fortress. The tactical uses of fortification are to effect a highly advantageous employment of one's own weapons while denying as much to the enemy. The Alamo, however, had not been built by tacticians. It had started out to be a mission, and in spite of minor military alterations it remained that and little more.

Through the industry of Captain Reuben Marmaduke Potter, a retired United States Army officer, a plan and complete description of the structure have been preserved.

Potter was a resident of Matamoras while the siege was
going on and for some while afterward. As a military man
he took an intense interest in the technical aspects of the
story and made several trips to inspect the fort. Fortunately
he had the ability to describe what he saw with precision.

The chapel, which is now almost all that is left of the
Alamo, faces west. It is a stone-masonry building seventy-
five feet long and sixty-two feet wide. The walls are four
feet thick and twenty-two and a half feet high. The windows
are walled over, a defensive measure which Potter believed
was owing to Cos or to some previous Mexican commander
of the post. The building was roofless except for a portion of
the western end and over the northern transept.

The inner court, as seen in 1836, would not have been
recognized by the Franciscans. The buildings where they
had lived and worked were gone. In place of the cloister
which once had led to them from the chapel there was a
twelve-foot wall, fifty feet long, connecting the northwest
corner of the chapel with the southeastern end of a long,
stone barracks lying along the east side of the plaza. The
southern wall of the inner court had vanished and was re-
placed with an entrenchment protected by a breastwork of
earth packed between two rows of wooden palisades. Running from the western end of the breastwork to the southwestern end of the long barracks just mentioned was a
four-foot wall, forming the west side of the inner court and
dividing it from the old mission plaza.

This plaza, whose walls composed the main defenses of
the Alamo, was an oriented rectangle, its long sides running
north and south. It was one hundred and fifty yards long
by fifty-four yards wide. The stone walls were two and
three quarters feet thick and ranged from nine to twelve feet
high, except for the four-foot stretch conterminous with

the inner court. The main plaza gate was at the southeast corner.

Five doors in the eastern wall opened into the barracks built along the outer side. These stone military quarters extended north of the inner court one hundred and eighty-six feet. They were two-story structures, eighteen feet wide and eighteen feet high, built in series like houses on a city block.

On the west side four doors led to as many isolated stone rooms. On the south side there were one-story barracks seventeen feet wide and extending for one hundred and fourteen feet. These were divided by a porte-cochere, the secondary gateway to the fort. The walls of all the barracks were two and a half feet thick. The buildings had thick, flat roofs made of cement supported by beams and planks.

That was almost all of the fort but not quite. North of the inner court and therefore in back of the two-story barracks on the east there was a small area enclosed, on its northern and eastern sides, by walls five to six feet high and two and three quarter inches thick. North of this again was a cattle pen defended on the north and east only by a picket fence.

Little technical knowledge is needed to see that the walls were neither thick enough to withstand prolonged bombardment, even from the cannon of the day, nor were they high enough to discourage assault by escalade. The weaknesses, however, ran far deeper than that. A fort is supposed to give protection to its garrison in addition to offering an obstacle to hostile arms. The Alamo furnished the minimum of cover possible to defenders attempting to shoot rifles or to service artillery.

There were a few loopholes in the barracks, but the walls were not supplied with loopholes, embrasures or crenellations. Riflemen had to stand on an earthen platform and shoot over the wall's flat top, head, shoulders and arms exposed. Similarly there were no provisions for the emplacement of cannon. These, too, had to shoot directly over the walls from mounds erected for their support.

It goes without saying that the Alamo was without bastions or any other structural feature designed to help the besieged garrison make it tough for the enemy. There were also—and this was worse—practically no outer works of any kind. A drainage ditch excepted, there were no moats, mines or pitfalls.

It was not to be expected that partisan fighters like Bowie and Travis, accustomed to maneuvering in the open, would know much about the complicated science of fortification, and there is no evidence that they did. The improvements supplied by the Texian garrison were few and primitive.

Before the Mexicans arrived they had built the earthwork guarding the inner court. Some of their other alterations weren't finished, or possibly even started, until the siege had begun. As already described, platforms of earth lined the inside of the walls for the benefit of riflemen. At certain points there was a secondary defense in the form of earthworks a few feet back from the walls. These were amplified here and there for the emplacement of batteries. Within the almost roofless chapel a scaffolding permitted men to shoot over the walls. A dirt ramp had been built there, too, so that cannon could be rolled into place aloft. Emergency measures consisted of putting barricades, each made of earth packed between stretched cowhides, behind the doors opening into the sundry barracks and isolated rooms. External fortification consisted solely of a palisade lunette protecting the porte-cochere entry in the middle of the southern wall.

To sum up, the judgment of the first military expert who wrote of the siege must stand. In the professional opinion of R. M. Potter, the Alamo had no real right to be considered a fort at all.

The armament was as inadequate as the passive defenses. The dirt ramp in the chapel reached a height of twelve feet in the apse. At this height rough embrasures had been made to accommodate a battery of three twelve-pounders. The middle one naturally pointed east, the two flanking pieces north and south respectively.

The combination trench and earthwork which protected the unwalled side of the inner court reached to the southeast corner of the plaza, where the main gate was located. Just behind the entrenchment at this point there was a battery of four four-pounders, pointing south. Behind the lunette protecting the porte-cochere there were two cannon, size not given, also pointing south. At the southern end of the plaza's west wall was the fortress' heaviest piece, an eighteen-pounder. At the center of the same wall was a twelve-pounder carronade. These guns pointed west to the river and the city.

At the western end of the north wall was an eight-pounder. There were two more in the center of the wall, all three pointing north. Over half of the east wall was covered by the inner court or was reinforced by the long, two-story barracks. There were no guns pointing east with the exception of the one from the battery in the apse of the chapel.

The total was fourteen guns. Sutherland mentioned that the Alamo had an arsenal including about thirty cannon but mentions that some were in a state of complete disrepair. Undoubtedly the fourteen were the only ones that were serviceable, for thrice the number and more could have been used. Not one was of a caliber such as a fort might be expected to have, and the efficiency of all was limited by the nature of their emplacements. Potter stated that the makeshift earth and palisade platforms on which the guns stood permitted hardly any maneuverability.

As for the guns themselves, they were unrifled, muzzle-loading cannon. Their designations, such as twelve-pounder, etcetera, referred to the weight of the cast-iron ball projectiles they were capable of throwing. To give a gauge, an eighteen-pounder had a caliber of 5.2 inches, but since the pieces weren't rifled, the diameter of the projectile was slightly less than that of the bore. Wadding was rammed in front of the ball to keep it snug against the powder charge. Then a touch hole in the breech was filled with a priming powder train. "Fire in the hole!" was the signal for everyone to stand clear.

Shrapnel had been in use for some time and is specifically mentioned as being used by the Mexicans in certain battles of the Texas Revolution. There is no evidence that the Alamo garrison had anything so modern in the way of ammunition, though a crude substitute was used. Against massed foot troops guns were loaded with scrap iron.

For frontiersmen, however, the deadliest weapon was not the cannon, in whose use they were generally unskilled, but the rifle. The modern weapon of the day was a muzzle-loading and therefore single shot weapon fired when the hammer struck a percussion cap inserted in a vent in the breech. This action not only ignited the charge but, as the hammer locked against the vent, it prevented the loss of gas pressure. The projectile was a true ball ammunition in the form of a spherical pellet, better than a half-inch in diameter, lapped in an oiled patch. It was the patch which made muzzle-loading rifles practical, for it sealed the bore, guarding against a waste of gas pressure through the grooves.

But although percussion cap ignition had been in use since about 1820, in 1836 it was only just beginning to take the place of flintlocks in the armies of the world. It is reasonable to believe then that there were many representatives of this older type of weapon in the Alamo. To fire such a rifle, powder had to be poured into a priming trap after the weapon was charged and loaded. When the cock fell, a piece of flint inserted in it struck a piece of metal and caused a spark. This ignited the powder train—or it was hoped that it would. Misfires were a commonplace, and in damp weather the powder in the exposed priming trap was apt to become soggy. Often it sputtered for agonizing moments before exploding the charge, making the holding of aim a difficult business.

Pistols were also likely to have either flintlock or percussion cap ignition. They ran in all sizes from snub-nosed sleeve weapons to the long horse pistols but were universally large caliber, short range weapons. Double-barreled pistols were not uncommon; but Colt had invented the percussion cap revolver just the year before, in 1835. It is improbable that any of the North Americans at Bexar owned one.

On the Texian side there is no mention of bayonets; their place for in-fighting was taken by the hunting knife. Many carried one that was more or less a replica of Bowie's famous weapon; others had given their own specifications to the making smith. Some undoubtedly carried tomahawks, for when the Texian army was being formed there was a proposal that this weapon should be included in a soldier's standard equipment. The tomahawk, however, was losing popularity as men moved west. Although in the forests of the east it doubled in brass as a handy tool, it wasn't of so much use to the horseback rangers of the plains country.

In addition to the arms already listed, there were a few swords. Typically, Travis carried one, and probably some of the officers of the volunteer companies brought them along. Some of them had uniforms, too, or what the fall campaign had left of them, but most of them wore buckskin and homespun.

Their supplies were of the same simple stamp. When the garrison withdrew to the Alamo they had taken along about thirty head of cattle and a hundred bushels of shelled corn abandoned by fleeing Mexican civilians. No other type of ration is referred to, though almost certainly they had that Mexican and military staple, the *frijole*. In the past, water had been supplied by a ditch which ran through the plaza. In the days of the Franciscans there had also been a well; but it must have become filled in, for it is stated that the garrison took the precaution of digging one. Being so near the river, they probably didn't have to go down very far.

So much for what they had to work with. Now for the garrison members themselves and the other inmates of the fort. The exact number present at the beginning of the siege is difficult to determine. In one of his letters midway in the battle, Travis said he had one hundred and fifty men; but a letter of Houston's explains that he only counted effectives, and Sutherland indicated there was something of a sick list. The various parties which joined the garrison before the siege total more than Travis' count, but adding them wouldn't give the sum either. Sutherland referred to some Texians who decided not to stay when they found Santa Anna was at hand. He mentioned, too, that of a group of Mexicans who joined the garrison February 23, most thought better of it and deserted within a few days.

Another factor that complicates the count is that an indefinite number of messengers, indefinite because the records are so conflicting on this point, were sent to various places in Texas in quest of assistance. All told, the original number, including the sick, lame and lazy, must have been close to two hundred. There were, likewise, about fifteen non-combatants, including the American wife of one of the garrison officers, several Mexican women, a group of children and the respective Negro servants of Bowie and Travis.

Although the detachment from Gonzales was to raise the proportion, only a minority among the defenders were genuine Texians in the sense that they had lived in Texas prior to participating in hostilities. Travis and Bowie were, of course, and so in all likelihood were most of the fifty or sixty men they brought with them. But the 104 on the roster before these arrived were mostly remnants of the New Orleans Grays and other volunteer organizations from the United States. Then there were Crockett's Tennesseans and strays of unknown provenance.

But whether Texians or not they were largely of one ilk. They were men who either by birth or by the choice of their parents or themselves had become identified with the old southwestern frontier of the United States, of which Texas was unofficially a part.

Honor rolls of the dead, which differ in quite a few particulars from the roster of those present at the beginning, have been compiled. It has been impossible to trace the previous vicissitudes of most of the rank and file, but in the majority of cases the native state or foreign country has been ascertained. These lists have minor points of disagreement, and therefore none can escape challenge, but they tell a little of who the men were.

To take one as an example; the birthplaces of 174 members

are listed. Those born beneath the Mason-Dixon Line and its extension as arranged by the Missouri Compromise numbered ninety-six. This does not include the only natives of Texas, of which there were nine, all Mexicans. Twenty-five hailed from the rest of the United States. Great Britain and Ireland supplied thirty-eight; continental Europe six.

It is further broken down. Once again, only an infallible ouija board could guarantee the accuracy of such a list, but it can be taken as correct on most counts. Tennessee, with twenty-nine names furnished the biggest contingent, followed by England with seventeen, Virginia with thirteen, Ireland with eleven, Kentucky and Mexico with nine each, South Carolina and Scotland with eight apiece; Georgia, Missouri and New York with seven each; Pennsylvania with six; Maryland, Louisiana and Germany with five apiece; North Carolina, Mississippi and Ohio with four each; Arkansas with three; Alabama, Massachusetts, Connecticut, New Jersey and Wales with two each; and Maine, New Hampshire and Denmark with one apiece.

Some of the volunteers have been accused, no doubt correctly, of being desperadoes. The majority of the garrison, however, were hunters, farmers, the more usual combination of both, and professional men. Not many had formal military experience, but there was nearly as much per capita rank as the *Iliad* could boast. An examination of the roster, in so far as it has been preserved, doesn't tell the full story in this respect.

Certain men listed as sergeants seem to have enjoyed, in practice, the title of captain. Crockett had no rank, but he was always called colonel and actually was in command of the detachment he brought with him, possibly more than that. Bonham was called colonel, though he was utilized mainly as a courier. The man who couldn't collect a fine-sounding title in the old Southwest either didn't have any friends or any imagination.

If that mirror seems humorous there's a true reflection in it. Men of aspiration, at that time and place, sincerely and unabashedly ennobled their peers and gravely accepted return tributes as no more than their due. There was not then a tendency to think meanly of life or people. Still less was there an inclination to the sickly humility whose basic premise is that no dog is better than another. If they obeyed orders it was as sovereigns obliging one another.

Well, the men of the Alamo earned the right to think of themselves what they might and to call themselves what they would, for they were unflinching in crisis. It would have been easy to skin over the walls at night. Couriers got through the enemy lines, and these woodsmen could have done likewise. Yet, with one exception, they all stayed.

Their motives can be approximated if not defined. Some had homes to protect, although they were in the minority. Some of the United States volunteers expected to settle in Texas after the war and so had a proprietary interest in the state. A stronger motive must have been loyalty to Bowie, Travis, or both. Then there was loyalty to the cause of independence as an ideal, coupled with a hatred of Mexicans, rooted either in bitter personal experience or the feeling that Texas had been stolen from the United States. Strongest of all must have been the individual feeling that it was impossible to quit on the team.

The fact that the team had been divided into regulars and volunteers, established Texians and newcomers from the States, was something not forgotten all at once. It wasn't until each faction had tested the grit of the other that there was complete unity. At first the dying Bowie's prestige was all that made the volunteers willing to obey a regular; but they soon saw that Travis was a leader after their fancy, too.

As for Travis, he was a good man, and he knew it. Once Bowie had given him the men, he had no doubt of his ability to keep them. Nor did he have any doubt as to his ability to keep the fort until help should arrive. He was exhilarated and proud at being in the position of holding the door to Texas.

On the second day of the siege, when he had just taken full command, following Bowie's collapse, he wrote the famous letter which showed his talent for passionate rhetoric. It also showed how in his own mind he had identified himself with the besieged fortress:

Commandancy of the Alamo, Bexar, Feby 24th, 1836.

To the People of Texas and All Americans in the World—

Fellow Citizens and Compatriots: I am besieged with a thousand or more of the Mexicans under Santa Anna. I have sustained a continual Bombardment and cannonade for 24 hours and have not lost a man. The enemy has demanded a surrender at discretion, otherwise, the garrison are to be put to the sword, if the fort is taken. I have answered the demand with a cannon shot, and our flag still waves proudly from the wall. *I shall never surrender or retreat*. Then, I call on you in the name of Liberty, of patriotism and everything dear to the American character, to come to our aid with all dispatch. The enemy is receiving reinforcements daily and will no doubt increase to three or four thousand in four or five days. If this call is neglected, I am determined to sustain myself as long as possible and die like a soldier who never forgets what is due his honor or that of his country. VICTORY or DEATH.

William Barret Travis
Lt. Col. Comd't.

While the courier was on the way to San Felipe with that message, the Mexicans began to close in. The walls of the Alamo had failed to yield to a long range cannonading by light field pieces. Now the true investment of the Alamo began.

X

THE TIGHTENING SIEGE

AT THE time Travis sent out his appeals for help the Texians had forfeited the ability to act as a body. The division in the government and the disruption of the army had so knotted the situation that everyone was hopelessly confused and entangled. The only course open was to start from scratch again, and a meeting of delegates was on the docket for March 1. Allowing for leap year day, that meant that the siege of the Alamo would be in its seventh day before the government could start to reorganize, let alone rebuild an armed force.

As things stood there was no administration to call a rescue expedition into being. The Governor still kept the title, but nobody else took it seriously. The council, which had ruined him, dismayed at the results of its actions, had folded up. There hadn't been a quorum since late January.

In the meantime, what of the old army and its four commanders? When General Houston, finding himself help-less, had asked for a leave of absence he wasn't just retiring to keep a chair warm while he watched. Always in close touch with the Cherokees, he had learned of Santa Anna's efforts to sick the Indians on the colonies, the attack to synchronize with the expected Mexican invasion. The General visited his former fellow-tribesmen and succeeded in winning a promise of neutrality from them. He thus averted a calamitous second front; but it meant that he was among those absent when the country of whose forces he was the rightful commander in chief was attacked. As it happened, the day he smoked the final pipe of peace with the Cherokees was the day Santa Anna marched into Bexar.

As to the three pretenders, the Matamoras Expedition they had insisted upon leading had gone up in smoke. Colonel Johnson and Dr. Grant couldn't get enough men to do business because the Texians had temporarily lost interest in their war, and Fannin had most of the volunteers. They decided therefore to utilize their remaining forces to hunt wild mustangs. Under the respective commanders two small columns moved west, intent upon this innocuous pursuit, just as the Mexicans were moving north. During the course of the siege, on February 27 and March 2 to be exact, the two bands were found and gobbled up by General Urrea, en route to attack Goliad. Johnson was one of four or five survivors, while Grant was slain.

Colonel Fannin had planned a sea-borne attack upon Mexico; but he couldn't get the shipping, and tentative plans for collaboration with Johnson and Grant didn't work out. In the end he retired to Goliad, piously protesting that he had no high military aspirations after all. Nevertheless, by virtue of having four hundred and some men, he was the *de facto* commander of the Texian army.

This was the man to whom perforce the defenders of the Alamo primarily turned for aid. As early as February 16, Colonel James Bonham had gone to Goliad with a request for some men to help replace the ones who had been lured away by talk of the Matamoras Expedition. On February 23, itself, Bonham had returned with a refusal; but by then new messengers had just been sent to Goliad telling of the actual presence of a hostile army. Travis felt sure that that would make a difference.

The siege commenced then with the garrison in a grimly cheerful mood. It would take pushing to hold what they had against the opposing odds, but they knew they could do it until help had time to arrive. They knew, too, that the enemy would attack unsparingly. Santa Anna could not afford to by-pass them and leave such a strong rallying point in his rear.

Santa Anna had no intention of doing so. The Mexicans had always been alive to the strategic importance of Bexar, and El Presidente had just had its value impressed forcibly upon him. The long march over desert country had just missed wrecking his army. Without a base of supplies in Texas he could go no farther, and the fertile Bexar region, with its huge herds of cattle, was the only likely quartermaster's hunting ground. When he proceeded against the colonies he could afford no such threat to his life lines as a fort in Texian hands. With his usual opportunism he sent a triumphant message back to Mexico City that he had captured Bexar, implying that he had it all. Then he set himself to make it a fact.

The general sequence of events can be followed in the diary of Colonel Almonte, taken from that officer when he was captured at San Jacinto. The information thus gained is eked out and in some cases enlarged upon by letters from Travis and by the statements of scouts who left the Alamo at various stages of the siege.

By late afternoon of the twenty-third the Mexicans had

two batteries of six-pounders on the far bank of the river, which at that point makes a horseshoe bend bulging westward. One battery was west and one southwest of the Alamo. They were replied to and put out of action by the fort's comparatively heavy eighteen-pounder, but by nightfall they were back in action. Travis wrote of a sustained cannonading and shower of bombs lasting twenty-four hours, a statement supported by Francisco Ruiz, alcalde of San Antonio de Bexar.

The Mexican guns were firing at a distance of a half-mile or more, a fair range for such light pieces, and too long a one for them to do much damage. They fired shells as well as shot; but time fire hadn't been heard of, and explosive ammunition was only effective against unprotected infantry. The shells exploded harmlessly, and the shot bounced off the stone mission walls.

Fortunately Santa Anna hadn't been able to drag along any guns of true siege caliber. If he had, the walls would never have lasted as long as they did in the first place, and in the second place he wouldn't have found it necessary to work his artillery as close to the fort as it eventually got. But if he didn't have heavy cannon, he did have quite a few light ones, and they rolled into Bexar with each new column.

During the twenty-fourth, another regiment of cavalry and three battalions of infantry swelled the Mexican forces. Santa Anna was then ready to begin his envelopment of the fort and made his first gesture toward the east bank of the river. A detachment of two to three hundred Mexicans crossed the San Antonio south of the Alamo and came up under cover of some buildings until they reached the open, about one hundred yards away. This was like drinks on the house for the Texian riflemen, who picked off several dozen before they retreated to shelter after persistent efforts to seat a battery.

Travis wrote jubilantly of the engagement, but it shows at once how green the Texians were at siegecraft and how much the town had been permitted to hamper the fort. Those buildings should never have been put there, but as long as they were, the garrison should have destroyed them before the battle began.

From then on the contest was like that of a desperate animal fighting off the implacable coils of a constrictor snake. The foray by day was followed by one at night. Again it was costly to the Mexicans; but though the hunters stole near enough to pot their game in the dark they didn't kill enough. Before daylight the enemy had seated a battery three hundred yards south of the Alamo and another a thousand yards to the southwest.

If the plan of the fort is borne in mind, the south side was the logical one to sound for weakness. Both gates were there and so, too, was the breastwork protecting the inner court. This dirt and wooden palisade arrangement, whose defense had been entrusted to Crockett, was potentially the most vulnerable point, all forms of attack considered, in the fortress.

The Mexicans were then on three sides, for cavalry were now encamped in force to the east of the fort. For quite a while Santa Anna did not try to emplace batteries to the east, whereas the Texians, be it recalled, only had one piece pointing in that direction. As both parties acted in concert in this respect, the east side must have been held peculiarly hard to attack. Of course the back of the chapel and the two-story barracks gave extra protection to about half of it. Meanwhile, the cavalry roosting on the low hills cut off the fort from the colonies.

One mounted engagement took place when some Texians sallied east for a skirmish on the twenty-sixth. Although not so recorded, it must have been a diversionary attack, designed to keep the cavalry out of mischief, for on the same day another engagement is mentioned wherein the Texians wrecked some buildings and burned others in the face of stiff opposition. In so doing they not only belatedly destroyed the cover the Mexicans had found most useful, but they supplied themselves with wood for scaffolding. Erected inside the roofless chapel this gave both sharpshooters and observers a fine vantage point.

The chapel, with its extra foot and a quarter of wall thickness, remained impervious to the cannonading throughout, but the constant battering was beginning to shake some of the lesser defenses. Still, at the end of four days the fort remained basically intact, and the Texians hadn't lost a man while inflicting heavy casualties on the Mexicans. The garrison was still strong and confident, but its members began to look to the east with increasing impatience. They had had a long trick on guard, and they needed a rest.

There were 150 able-bodied men, and all who could move were considered ready for duty. They had, including the plaza, the inner court and the chapel, a total front of nearly five hundred yards to defend. Subtracting from duty strength the four or five men needed to man each of the fourteen cannon, there were well under a hundred left for riflemen, ammunition carriers, ordnance repairmen and the numerous details indispensable to the operation of a military post in combat or out. For officers there was no relief, for the artillerymen no relief, for the men on special duty no relief, day or night. All ate and slept—when they did sleep—at their posts, their loaded weapons beside them.

Santa Anna had learned almost the exact strength of the

garrison from Mexicans remaining in Bexar, and part of his strategy was aimed at wearing the Texians down by keeping them constantly on the alert. There were feints by day and noisy raids by night; and under cover of both the Mexicans doggedly wove their network of trenches nearer. Day and night the ever closer batteries kept firing.

The cannonading of the Texians, on the other hand, had slackened up after the first day or so. Sutherland stated that the Alamo was well supplied with powder; but the evidence is to the contrary. What looked like a great deal of powder to a physician didn't turn out to be so much, what with fourteen cannon making demands upon it. The eighteen-pounder alone took twelve pounds for each shot. The supply must have dwindled alarmingly, for Almonte took note of the fact that the garrison was firing sparingly, obviously hording.

For breakfast in the Alamo there was corn and beef, for lunch corn and beef, for supper beef and corn. The ninety or so bushels of corn and twenty to thirty head of cattle mentioned by Travis in one of his letters was, he stated, almost their entire stock of food. With little to help stretch it, these items went fast, and short commons was added to the troubles of the defenders. As foreseen, the Mexicans tried to, and partially succeeded in, blocking the ditch which had supplied the fort with water in the past. Fortunately the well which was dug proved adequate.

February 27 was highlighted by several developments. The Mexicans tried to bridge the river, and thirty were killed before they decided it was a bad idea. During the day the third column of Santa Anna's army arrived. By Potter's finding there were now nine batteries trained or ready to be trained on the Alamo. Meanwhile, by that, the fifth day of the siege, not one man had arrived to strengthen the garrison, nor had the Mexican cavalry, posted to watch for reinforcements, been disturbed at their vigil. Not so much as a courier had come through the hostile lines to report what was going on in the rest of Texas. Once more Travis sent Colonel Bonham to Colonel Fannin at Goliad.

Bonham got past the Mexicans and so, it would seem, did all the other couriers. There were a dozen or so in all, and there is no record of any of them being caught; but they were frontiersmen. If they hadn't been able to take care of themselves they wouldn't have lived as long as they did in a land where Indian war parties still swarmed. Two, as shall be related, returned to report their success or the lack of it; but most of them vainly waited to guide rescue expeditions that were never formed until it was too late.

The waiting in ignorance grew to be as much of a strain as the sleeplessness and the fatigue caused by the continuous bombardment, the constant alarms and excursions. And Santa Anna increased the pressure.

The Texians never let down, but by February 28 they were almost completely boxed. The Mexicans put a battery in an old mill to the northwest. Thus they had the fort covered by guns on the southeast, the south, the southwest, the west and the northwest. Only directly north and to the east where the cavalry hovered were there as yet no field guns.

Directly south, as has been seen, a battery was only three hundred yards off, and a system of creeping entrenchments was shortening the distance night by night. Yet there was still no word from the east on leap year day, the seventh day of the siege, and Travis again sent out a pair of messengers in the persons of Captain Juan Seguin, commander of the small Mexican contingent of volunteers, and one of his men.

By then it was wrongly feared that none of the other couriers had got through, and it was hoped that Captain Seguin's Spanish might get him past the enemy where woodcraft had failed. Luckily, the Captain lived to relay to Potter an account of what happened.

Seguin had no mount in the Alamo but borrowed one from Bowie. For the first few days of the siege the latter had left his sick bed from time to time in order to lend encouragement and to make sure the volunteers were cooperating with Travis; but by February 29, when Seguin asked for his horse, Bowie was so far gone with fever that he hardly knew him. However, he acceded to the Captain's request.

Giving word of their mission to a Texian outpost, Seguin and his companion slipped into no-man's land and rode leisurely eastward. A clear night eventually revealed them to a roving cavalry patrol, whose leader ordered them to approach. To this Seguin agreed, his accent allaying suspicion. The troopers didn't know they had hailed any but a couple of wandering *vaqueros* until, when he was just about abreast of them, the Captain dug in his spurs.

Both he and the other courier were well mounted, and they had the bulge on the enemy. The pistols missed them in the night, and they were soon lost to pursuit in a patch of woods. In the clear, they turned toward Goliad, but Bonham could have told them it was a fruitless trip. Around then the hard-riding colonel was receiving assurance that no help would be given the Alamo from Fannin.

It would have been better for the memory of that commander if he had done nothing at all; but he actually started for Bexar and quit. Three or four miles out of Goliad a supply wagon had broken down, and this—as taken from his own statement—led him to believe that the expedition was not feasible. He held a conference on the spot, and it was decided to turn back.

To give Fannin what justice is coming to him, his hundreds could not of themselves have defeated the thousands under Santa Anna. But such a force would have served as a core around which other Texians would have quickly rallied. He did nothing, and, except for the men of the Alamo, the state's war effort remained in a coma. It could be argued that he felt he must not weaken the defenses of Goliad, but when it came to the pinch he didn't defend the place anyhow. Even a portion of his men would have helped Travis, for a troop of mounted frontiersmen could have been a harrying force capable of lifting much of the pressure from the fortress at Bexar.

As a matter of fact, a temporary division of Mexican forces was created as it was. Mexican scouting, aided by native spies, was so good that Santa Anna knew Fannin had intended to come to the relief of the Alamo and sent a strong force eastward to intercept him. Finding there would be no relief expedition, the Mexican troops returned to Bexar, and Santa Anna was able to employ his full strength in consummating the siege.

Meanwhile, Seguin was spared making the whole trip to Goliad, for when almost there he met one of Fannin's officers. The latter warned him he was wasting his time and advised him to try Gonzales. Without delaying, the Captain rode for that town, whither Bonham had preceded him. The Colonel, like the Captain, arrived late, for the men of Gonzales, alone of all Texians, had set out for the Alamo.

As Bexar was not a Texian town, Gonzales, seventy miles to the east, was the most westerly North American community of any size. It was for this reason that so many messengers had been sent there, although one other was undoubtedly influential. The settlement was known as a strong-hold of independence, a reputation established when the "Come and Take It" banner greeted the Mexican troops who had tried to seize the town's lone cannon.

Sutherland and Smith had reached Gonzales by the night of February 24—they would have reached it earlier, but the doctor had to favor his leg—and a third courier may have arrived before them. Riders from Gonzales had since relayed messages on several occasions to San Felipe and Washington. The town was, therefore, well posted on the progress of the siege. It should also be borne in mind that the town was well posted on the state of affairs within the Texian settlements.

By February 29, the citizenry of Gonzales knew that Fannin had decided against action at Bexar. By the twenty-ninth they knew there would be no organized effort to relieve the beleaguered fort until a new government was formed at the Washington conference of March 1. By that time, too, they knew that, in the absence of leadership, there would be no such rallying of volunteers as had been hoped for. Having waited vainly to become a part of an expedition, a band of Gonzales men set out by themselves.

This was a great doing. These men knew that the help they brought would of itself be entirely insufficient. They knew that timely aid from the rest of Texas was an unlikelihood. They understood the weakness of the Alamo and the strength of the Mexicans. But they had received a call from friends in straits, and they would not ignore it.

Captain George C. Kimball was in command of the thirty-two men from Gonzales and the adjacent district who rode forth on that desperate mission. John W. Smith, a good man himself, undertook to guide them through the Mexican lines and past the outposts the Texians always stationed as protection against a surprise night attack. They reached the Alamo after dark on March 1.

Remarkably, all got through, and the only one scathed was shot in the foot by a hasty Alamo sentry. Some historians declare that Santa Anna deliberately let the detachment through, so that he could have a bigger bag of Texians in the end; but that not only reads like nonsense, it is nonsense. There were already more expert riflemen in the fort than El Presidente wanted there. They were picking off his men by the dozens daily and were, on the whole, much more effective than the fort's artillery in making the Mexicans keep their distance. When the Alamo recruited thirty odd new marksmen it is certain that Santa Anna had no part in it.

The garrison was tremendously cheered by the arrival of the newcomers. They needed something to cheer them. Here and there the walls were beginning to crumble under the steady pounding. The night Seguin left an attempt to smash a link in the artillery chain by attacking a battery to the northwest had been repulsed. That same night a Mexican infantry battalion had dug in to the east of the fort. So by the morning of March 1, the day the men from Gonzales arrived, the Alamo was menaced by assault from almost all points of the compass.

If *Col. Crockett's Exploits and Adventures in Texas* is without any factual source, it must be conceded to be, in its passages dealing with the siege, a forceful piece of creation. True or not, it gives a plausible glimpse of what life for the garrison was like in the mid-stage of the battle. The picture presented is one of frontier paladins making sallies more or less on their own initiative, taking turns at sharpshooting for the daily bag of Mexicans, joking and swapping yarns—and wondering when help was coming and whether they could hold out until it did.

Up to this point Santa Anna had been operating deliberately, getting his troops into position as they arrived and moving them forward as opportunity offered. Once he found himself under fire when the Alamo's eighteen-pounder got the range of the building he had commandeered for his headquarters. Yet prior to February 29 he directed the disposition of troops from a distance. But on leap year day and on March 1, as Colonel Almonte noted, he made thorough personal inspections of the battlefield.

During the course of one of them he was observed and shot at by the garrison, but the range was too great for the rifles of the day. As for the cannon, they were hardly fired at all at that stage. The Texians were running way short on powder, and they were holding their artillery fire for the assault they knew they would sooner or later have to face.

Santa Anna decided he wasn't yet ready, however, and as a result of his reconnoitering, the Mexican lines squeezed closer yet to the Alamo. On March 2, Almonte reported, Mexican scouts had discovered a road "within pistol shot" of the fort and were guarding it to prevent the going and coming of couriers. The fact that it hadn't been discovered before suggests that it was a roadway worn deep in the ground like the one which trapped Napoleon's cavalry at Waterloo, but the Colonel didn't elaborate. In any case, his belief that the Mexicans had found the only safe route for couriers proved wrong.

At the moment that notation was being scribbled in Almonte's diary, Colonel James Butler Bonham was making his ride of gallantry from Gonzales. With Fannin's note of refusal in his pocket he had gone to Gonzales to make an appeal there, only to find that Captain Kimball and his men had left on February 29. In the two days which had since elapsed, hopelessness had immeasurably deepened as far as timely relief for the garrison was concerned. He was told that he had already done everything that he could and that reaching the Alamo—if he lived to reach it—was suicide. His reply was that he owed it to Travis to report the failure of his mission.

Bonham was of a notable South Carolina family. At some time in his youth he had gone to school with Travis, so that friendship was added to the military loyalty which impelled him on his final journey. At the time he had been in Texas less than three months, having first arrived there on December 12, 1835. Undoubtedly, he came with the express purpose of serving the struggling state, for he immediately offered himself to the army. Accepted, he was commissioned a lieutenant. He made a favorable impression upon Houston, who wrote a letter stating that Bonham was qualified to be a major. Apparently this didn't carry any more weight with the council than did most of the General's other opinions, and it is unlikely that Bonham was officially anything but a lieutenant in the Texian army. It didn't matter. Somewhere, in a manner that seems mysterious today but that then was a commonplace, he had picked up a colonelcy. Once a colonel always a colonel in the old Southwest. He was never called anything else.

Like Travis he was a lawyer; and he must have been an accomplished scout in addition to a tireless horseman. Capping his three hundred and fifty mile trip, covered in well under five days and including two sneaks through the enemy lines, he appeared at the gates of the Alamo, horse and all. He was comfortably ahead of the pursuing Mexican patrol, whose leader probably had some difficulty in explaining how a man could get past him. It was eleven o'clock in the morning.

The message from Goliad was the end of hope as far as

Travis was concerned. But Bonham had also brought the only direct word of what was going on in the eastern colonies. The conference at Washington was being held as scheduled, and it was believed that the party in favor of independence would win the upper hand. Yet it would inevitably take days to form a new government, and it would never be formed if Santa Anna was free to sweep forward. Travis was more determined than ever to hold on as long as he could.

At the same time he felt he owed it to his men to tell them exactly what the score was and to allow them their own option in the matter. It has been the practice to consider this episode apocryphal, because the deserter who reported it was considered a legendary figure. The existence of the man, along with proof of his membership in the Alamo garrison, has, however, recently been established.

Louis Rose was the fellow's name. He was one of Napoleon's mercenaries, who emigrated to America following the emperor's downfall. He is described as having been a pretty rough citizen; brave enough, too, when he could see reason to be. Yet it is not in the creed of the mercenary to die for lost causes. He lived to recount, with an impersonal acceptance of the difference between his point of view and that of the rest of the garrison, the following episode to the Texian family which first sheltered him after his flight.

The night of March 3, when he had had time to digest what he had learned from Bonham, Travis called together all that could be spared from sentry duty and told them flatly that in his opinion there was almost no chance of getting relief before Santa Anna launched his assault. On the other hand, he gave them all the reasons why he thought it was imperative for them to continue to defend the fort, nevertheless. Rose, who spoke broken English, could not pretend to give Travis' speech, and the man who took the story from him did an indifferent job of dubbing it in. He used too many flowers and not enough salt to catch the flavor of Travis' rhetoric. However, the speech was made, and no doubt it was a humdinger.

The commander's next act has been challenged because it recalled Pizarro, as if that conquistador was the first or the last man to use a sword to draw lines with. Or maybe Travis did remember Pizarro, who was also a man of dramatic instincts. At any rate, at the conclusion of his speech he declared that he would coerce no man but that those who elected to stay must make the decision on the spot, so that he would know just whom he could count upon. He then made a mark on the ground with his sword, stepped across it and asked who would join him.

Some jumped, some went more slowly, some hesitated. Crockett was one of the first across. Because of his influence Bowie had been brought to the assemblage on a stretcher. To some on the honest side of the line he now called weakly: "Boys, I can't make it by myself, but I'd appreciate it if some of you would give me a hand." In his wake, the rest of the garrison then stepped over, with the sole exception of Rose, who could see no percentage in it. Nobody tried to interfere with him as he dropped down on the outer side of the wall and escaped.

The men of the Alamo never did learn that independence had been declared and that the Texas Nation was being formed. But they were its only shield at the time, and from March 3 on they were consciously dedicated men.

Nevertheless, more to prod his fellow-Texians into speedy action than with any hope of being rescued, Travis sent out, on that same night of March 3, one last appeal, addressed directly to the delegates at Washington. This letter was not written in triumphant exaltation like the one of February 24; its spiritual ink was a resigned determination:

> . . . I look to the colonies alone for aid; unless it arrives soon I shall have to fight the enemy on his own terms. I will, however, do the best I can . . . and although we may be sacrificed . . . the victory will cost the enemy so dear, that it will be worse for him than defeat. I hope your honorable body will hasten reinforcements. . . . Our supply of ammunition is limited. . . . God and Texas. Victory or Death.

The letter was entrusted to the redoubtable John W. Smith. Bonham was the last man to join or rejoin the garrison. Smith was the last Texian to leave the fort alive.

That night, the men of the Alamo made their last recorded sally. That very night, too, the Mexicans moved another battery. Daylight on March 4 showed Mexican cannon menacing the north wall directly. By the fifth, at least, these guns had advanced to what Almonte again described as being within musket range.

Thus murderously close, this battery finally brought about what Santa Anna had been trying to accomplish for eleven days. A sizable breach was battered in the east end of the plaza's north wall.

XI

THE FINAL ASSAULT

WHEN he had at last breached the fortress, Santa Anna did something of which only a very subtle man would have been capable. He did nothing for some hours.

The men of the Alamo, who had met every test exacted by danger and fatigue, were tripped and trapped. A barrage, laying down the carpet for an attack, they could have endured as only one more call upon their fortitude. They were keyed to violence, ready for it in all its forms. Cannon fire had been so continual that it had become accepted as normal. Under stress they could have held themselves together, but peace and rest temporarily dissolved them.

At nightfall, on March 5, the firing suddenly ceased. It was only when no more bombs exploded and no more cannon balls thudded against the shattering defenses that they knew how exquisitely worn out they were. In ten days of ceaseless fighting there had been no more than snatches of rest for ill-fed men. Whatever the Mexicans might or might not be planning, they had to have sleep now that it was possible. With only a few sodden men keeping watch out of dead eyes, they slept where they were.

Just what was going on behind the Mexican lines has been preserved, officially by Colonel Almonte, unofficially by Ben, an American Negro who cooked for Santa Anna throughout the siege. Infinitely more important than the reports of either of these, of course, is Santa Anna's general order.

As early as the night of March 4, by Almonte's account, Santa Anna called a staff meeting at which he declared his intention of making a full-scale assault upon the Alamo. Even with a breach beaten in one of the walls, some of his officers did not like the idea. Texian marksmanship had cost them heavy casualties at long range, and they didn't believe it wise to move any closer until the garrison was more at a disadvantage. They were for following up their former tactics until the walls were down, exposing the defenders to point-blank grape fire.

Santa Anna overruled all objections. His reasons, if he gave his staff any, were not recorded, but they are not hard to imagine. He knew through spies that the Alamo was the only obstacle which intervened between his army and the rebellious North Americans he yearned to punish. He knew, too, that they were currently holding a meeting with a view to reorganizing their resistance. Now, before they could pull themselves together, was the time to hit them.

As it was, he had already lost ten days before this fort, and every day was money in the bank for Texas. Then there was sheer anger at the interference with well-laid plans. If the Alamo hadn't proved so unexpectedly tough the Mexicans would by then have already reached the Sabine, and the revolution would have been over.

Ben, the cook, reported a conversation between Santa Anna and Almonte in the course of which the latter stated that the cost would be high. To this the former retorted that he didn't care how many casualties there were, the Alamo had to be taken. As a result of his resolve his chief of staff issued the following order on March 5:

For the private information of Generals of Division and Corps Commanders:

. . . His excellency, the General in Chief, directs that by four o'clock tomorrow morning the attacking columns shall be stationed within gunshot of the first line of entrenchments for the purpose of making the assault, upon the signal given by His Excellency, which will be the sounding of the bugle from the north battery.

The first column will be commanded by Gen. Don Martin Perfecto de Cos. . . . This column will be composed of the Aldamas battalion of regulars—with the exception of the company of Grenadiers—and the three first companies of the volunteer battalion of San Luis.

The second column will be commanded by Gen. Don Francisco Duque [called a colonel by Almonte]. . . . This column will be composed of the three remaining companies of the San Luis battalion of volunteers.

The third column will be led by Col. Don Jose Maria Romero. . . . It will be composed of the infantry companies, in full force, of the Matamoras and Jimines battalions of regulars.

The fourth column will be led by Col. Don Juan Morelos. . . . This column will be composed of the cavalry companies of the Matamoras and Jimines regulars and the San Luis battalion of volunteers.

The General in Chief will, at the proper time, designate the points against which the attacking columns will operate. . . .

The reserve will be composed of the battalions of Sappers and Miners, and the five companies of the grenadiers of the Matamoras, Jimines and Aldamas battalions of regulars and of the Toluca and San Luis battalions of volunteers. . . .

The first column will be provided with ten scaling ladders, two crow bars, and two axes. The second will be provided with the same quantity; the third with six, the fourth with two. Men carrying ladders will sling their guns over their shoulders. . . .

Grenadiers and the cavalry companies will be supplied with six packs of cartridges and the infantry companies four, with two extra flints. . . . All caps will be provided with chin straps. . . .

The men composing the attacking column will retire to rest at sundown, preparatory to moving at midnight. . . .

Arms, particularly bayonets, will be put in the best condition.

When the moon rises the musketeers of the San Luis battalion of volunteers will retire to their quarters. . . . Other units will retire at sundown.

The cavalry under the command of General Don Joaquin Ramirez y Sesma will occupy the Alameda and will saddle up there at three o'clock in the morning. It will be their duty to watch camp and to prevent the escape of anyone. . . .

The numerical strength of the attacking force was not computed, but it can be given with reasonable accuracy. The strength of one of the battalions, at the time it took part in the assault, is definitely given at eight hundred men. As there are five battalions mentioned, it can fairly well be assumed that about four thousand men stood by for the action. From the toughness of the fight it can also be assumed that all four thousand were called upon to participate.

It will have been noted that there is a curious discrepancy between the strength of the other columns and that of column two. Although commanded by a general, this is listed as being composed of only three companies, whereas the third, for instance, was made up of the better part of two battalions. It seems likely that the Toluca Battalion of Volunteers, specifically cited as having taken a prominent part, but represented in the order only by its company of grenadiers, was unintentionally omitted from the clause dealing with column two. It should be remarked, also, that the cavalry under General Sesma, detailed for patrol duty, is a different body of horsemen from those under Colonel Morelos, designated as the fourth column, and should not be counted as part of the assault force. The cartridges referred to were not the metal contrivances now in use but folds of paper holding measured charges.

When Mexican firing ceased as night came down on March 5, Travis ordered his outposts to take their stations, and three exhausted men went out of the fort to keep watch against surprise. They were presumably relieved before three o'clock in the morning, but their successors were in no better shape. Now that they had let down, it would take days of solid rest to restore their faculties to keenness. Only movement could keep them alert at all, and as outposts they had to lie low, straining eyes and ears no longer in quick contact with the brain.

How long each held out can't be known. Scouts, woodsmen, hunters and Indian fighters, they succumbed to the need for sleep no man can push away forever and lay there as helpless as fledglings in a ground nest. One by one, it is known as certainly as if it was recorded, they were dealt with by Mexican scouts crawling up on them in the dark. A knife in the right spot and a hand on the throat to deny the sleeper even the bark of death, and it was all over. None of them lived to give a peep of warning.

There was, however, of all the garrison one man who remained awake, or who happened to awake, and who noticed a stirring at the rim of vision permitted by the light of a pale moon. He raised a shout which brought the Texians struggling out of the sleep that drowned them. That shout blended with the bugle call which was the signal for the charge. With cheers for Santa Anna the Mexicans dashed at the walls from all four sides.

Just as they were in full career the bugle sounded a different note, one which was taken up and swelled by the bands assembled at Santa Anna's headquarters. Waiting in the shadow of a blood-red banner, itself a symbol of no quarter, El Presidente had ordered the sounding of the *deguello*. This word means "assassin," and the call was an order to butcher without mercy or discrimination. Its military history dated back to the savage wars between the Spanish and the Moors. To the Mexicans, aware of its tradition, it was an elixir inspiring frenzied brutality.

The cheers for Santa Anna changed to less articulate but much more meaningful cries. Through the night, the battalions came with a rush, the men with the scaling ladders in the front rank, the rest flashing their bayonets at the end of readied muskets.

Travis, with a commander's burden to make his sleep uneasy, had been about the first to hear the shout of alarm. He sprang from his headquarters, shouting, as quoted by his Negro body servant, who dutifully followed him: "The Mexicans are on us; give 'em Hell, boys!" He himself took his stance by the battery guarding the north wall, the one which had been breached at one end.

The Texians had very nearly been caught napping in the most literal sense, but a minute or so of warning was all they needed. All weapons had, of course, been loaded before they started to take it easy. Now they waited, not taking a chance of missing in the night, until the attackers were massed close to the walls. Then they gave it to them, blasting holes in the live lines with cannon loaded with small shot and scrap iron. At the same time the rifles fired, and after them the pistols. In his supposed diary, Crockett asserted that Santa Anna would have "snakes to eat before he can get over the wall." By the proxy of his men he, indeed, ate snakes, rammed down his throat.

The scaling ladders were never planted that first time. In fact the Mexicans were lucky to be able to carry them away. Only the south column actually reached the wall it was headed for. Meanwhile the column at the north had been blasted back, and those to the east and west were wavering. Seeing themselves left alone, the south column gave up, too. The officers tried to hold their troops, but a second cannon volley turned wavering into a rout. The carnage was terrible, and officer casualties were particularly heavy. General Francisco Duque, leading the north column, had been badly wounded but continued to try to rally his command. In the eventual break for safety he was trampled to death by his own men.

The Texians had every reason for cheering but not long to indulge in it. The Mexicans, their flight notwithstanding, were soldiers and brave ones. In spite of the bloody repulse, their officers were soon able to talk them up to it, and by dawn their ranks were reformed. Once again the charge was sounded, followed by the *deguello,* beating the air with its cry for murder.

As before, the south column made the best showing, actually throwing its scaling ladders against the wall. And as before, the north column recoiled and those of the east and west were beaten back. It happened that in retreating, however, the east column swerved to the left while that of the west veered to its right. Whatever the reason, military or instinctive, the result was a massing of troops to the north. That routed column, encouraged by the unexpected reinforcements, stopped fleeing. Some of the officers were opportunists enough to weld all three forces into a body, and they came on once more. They reached the wall on the return trip, but there the gun fire broke them before they could use their ladders. The fighting on the south had grown even hotter meanwhile, for there the Mexicans had swarmed up the ladders and gained a foothold on the wall. Rifle butts and bowie knives forced them off, and no one followed the first hardy few. North and south, then, the attackers gave way and hastened out of range of Texian rifle fire.

But the Mexicans hadn't been beaten as easily as they had been the first time, and their officers had learned something. It was a while before they could put their new knowledge to use, though. The two attacks had been very costly. The participating units had to be resorted and checked over, and the men had to be given a chance to pull themselves together. It is very likely that the reserve was called upon at that time, for the heavy losses indicate the necessity. All in all it was several hours later, eight o'clock or thereabouts in the morning, before the attackers got around to risking another try.

Miraculously, the Texians hadn't lost a man the first ten days of the siege at any rate, and not many of the garrison had fallen while repelling the first two charges. Yet the assaults had cost them most of their powder and ammunition reserve. Their reserve of energy was likewise running out, and it was clear that they would soon be called on to draw upon it again. They could tell by the activity in the enemy lines that the Mexicans were not yet ready to call it quits; but when nothing happened right away most of the defenders went to sleep again.

Those detailed for sentry duty could see the red flag on San Fernando Cathedral and the bustle around Santa Anna's headquarters, now only five hundred yards away. Being human, they doubtless glanced at the eastern horizon from time to time on the frazzled chance of seeing a rescue expedition, but only the familiar Mexican cavalry patrols were in sight. Then at last they could see the infantry deploying into position once more. Roused from their last sleep, the men of the Alamo picked up their rifles, stood beside their cannon and grimly waited.

With the massed bands playing the cut-throat *deguello* from the spot where Santa Anna watched, the Mexicans swept forward from all four sides for a third time. It looked like a repetition of the other two assaults, but it wasn't. When the east and west columns were checked by the fire of the garrison, they swerved to the north, not by coincidence but by preconceived plan. The north column, which had been holding back, rushed forward, allowing those of the east and west to fall in behind as support.

The Texians made hash out of the front ranks, but only three cannon were trained northward. The Mexicans died by squads, but the force was so large that its impetus wasn't weakened. The men behind drove the men in front forward, and those who lived found themselves under the walls of the Alamo.

Jammed so close, they were safe from the cannon; but that was not the worst of the situation, so far as the defenders were concerned. By daylight, a man mounting the wall to shoot down at the troops trying to place scaling ladders was a fair target for the Mexican soldiers in the rear. As a Mexican general put it in a report of the battle, a Texian on the wall "could not live for an instant."

So the ladders were thrown up against the north wall for the first time. The combined forces of the east, west and north columns had between fifteen and twenty ladders used against a fifty-four-yard wall, breached at one end. The defenders could not normally have afforded ten riflemen for such a stretch, though the only partially repaired breach had made it necessary to thin the defense of the other walls, putting the bodies of men to hold where stone had failed. Undoubtedly, too, riflemen assigned to the west and east walls had largely moved to the north when they saw the columns which had confronted them do so.

The south column had for a third time forced its way

to the wall, but the fight there was a stalemate. It was at the north that the decisive struggle was taking place.

Up the ladders came the Mexicans, under cover of rear rank musket fire, and they surged through the breach at the earthwork behind it. Once the attackers were high enough to scramble on the walls, however, their comrades had to hold their fire, and the men of the Alamo sprang to meet them, knife and tomahawk against bayonet.

A wall whose top surface is only two and three quarters feet wide isn't much of a platform for a hand to hand fight. Its narrowness hampered the desperate garrison, but it was even more of a handicap to the attackers. A foothold in depth was impossible, so the men coming off the ladders had no protection for the awkward moment when they shifted from using their hands from climbing to using them for fighting. That moment was fatal to many, and the few that cleared the wall were shot or knifed before they could get their balance. Eastward, by the breach, the slaughter was even worse, as frontier rifles brought down every man trying to pick his way over the rubble.

For that few minutes, and for the last time, the defenders held their own, holding the Mexicans off at the south and throwing them back at the north. There from the breach to the westward angle the wall was kept in spite of the tremendous pressure; but that very pressure squeezed some of the Mexicans so that they overlapped the wall and found themselves facing the west one again.

They attacked at that point, and others eagerly peeled off the rear ranks to join them. Just as the Texians knew that they had to stand then or go down, the Mexicans knew that they had to make this assault good or swallow a decisive defeat.

The Alamo men were great and terrible that day, one

and all terrific in their try for victory and their secondary will to make the enemy pay a ruinous price for success; but it took brave men to keep fighting them. It took well-disciplined men and determined leadership to accept the casualties the Mexicans endured that day, and to keep coming back for more. Of a strength of 800 men, the Toluca Battalion was reported to have lost 670 during the three attacks. This battalion supplied the shock troops for the final one, and most of its men fell on the way to or at the north wall.

That continued to hold, but the outnumbered Texians, desperately occupied, weren't able to switch enough men fast enough to meet the new attack from the northern end of the west wall. Scaling ladders thrown down at the north were brought around. While the first men up were being killed by the few defenders, the men behind pushed past and dropped to the ground. The Texians guarding the breach found themselves taken from behind. They had to give way, and the attackers poured through the hole in the wall. To keep from being surrounded the men on the wall itself had to abandon it, and the Mexicans came over by platoons.

Just behind the wall was the earthwork supporting the battery of three guns, two in the middle and one at the west end. It was here that Travis, who had been in personal command of the north wall throughout, died holding on. The guns swept the wall in this sector for the last time, then the crews were never allowed a chance to reload. In the expressive phrase of Travis' man, Joe, "the Mexicans poured over the walls like sheep" and rushed the battery.

Having emptied his own pistol, Joe had jumped down from the earthwork but hesitated a moment to see how his master was faring. Travis was down when Joe turned to look, mortally wounded, as was later found to be the case, by a shot in the head. But the will which had steered the defense of the Alamo for twelve days still had one spark left. His pistol had been fired, but he had drawn his sword before he was hit, and he still kept his grip on it when he staggered to his feet. The first wave of Mexicans had just mounted the earthwork, an officer in the van. That officer, seeing an adversary who held his ground, sprang for him, but Travis' dying impulse was quicker. He drove his sword through the Mexican, then fell with him.

The line of soldiers behind ran over both officers, and Joe ran to take cover. By then the northern section was cleared of all but dead Texians. At about this time the hard-pressed defenders of the south wall had learned of the disaster. To avoid being shot in the back they had withdrawn, letting in more hundreds of Mexicans. The Alamo had been taken, but the bitterest phase of the struggle was yet to be fought.

The plaza, comprising by far the largest part of the fort, was in enemy hands. Remaining to the Texians were the long barracks on the east side of it, the smaller barracks on the south, the four stone rooms on the west side, the inner court and the chapel. All of these in turn became battle grounds.

There was no thought of parley on either side. The Texians never doubted that there was only a choice between being slain in combat and being assassinated. The Mexicans on their part were worked up to a pitch of rage which admitted no pause to talk things over. The pitiless wail of the *deguello* kept telling them what was expected of them, even if they hadn't had vengefulness to drive them. Their ranks had suffered horrible losses. They had seen their comrades slaughtered by the hundreds while they had futilely beat against the walls. Now they had the deadly defenders where they wanted them. They were obsessed with a maniacal hatred balancing the demonic resolution of the garrison. The fury of the combat didn't abate until the last man of the Alamo was bayoneted as he lay dying.

This took some doing even before the plaza was cleared. Most of the living defenders found a place to put their backs against, but some were caught in the open. They were over-powered one by one, but first they smashed the heads of their attackers with gun butts, ripped Mexicans open with knives, chopped them with tomahawks, or throttled them to death even as bayonets entered their own bodies.

The eighteen-pounder, guarding the approach from the west, hadn't played much of a part in the climactic third assault, but one group of Texians manned it even as the enemy flooded the plaza. Lifting it from its emplacement and swinging it around, they turned it on the attackers, mowing them down with a scatter charge. Before the Mexicans knew just what had hit them, the piece had been re-loaded and fired again, but that was for the last time. Standing on the unprotected platform, the gunners were felled by a fusillade of musket fire.

Only Texian corpses remained in the open, but defenders barricaded in the barracks were dropping Mexicans as fast as they could fire and reload. The battle at this point re-solved into a dozen separate engagements, pitting a platoon or so against the half-dozen or dozen defenders at bay in the various buildings and parts of buildings.

There was no communication between the five subdivi-sions of the long barracks or between the four quarters of the shorter barracks against the south wall. All told, thirteen doors, counting the four giving entry to the four small build-ings to the east, had to be beaten down by battering rams, crowbars and axes. Behind the doors were the semicircular barricades, described by Potter, made by packing earth between series of stretched cowhides.

So it was ram and thud till the doors splintered, with the defenders shooting from loopholes and windows and dropping as many Mexicans as they could in the meantime. Then when the doors shivered and gave inwards, the price of entry was death for the first attackers shoved in from behind. These were brought down by rifle and pistol fire, but after the first volley there was no chance to reload. It was a hand to hand encounter with the odds ten and twenty to one. Eventually the Texians were shot or overpowered at their makeshift ramparts, or else they were forced back into a corner of a room, there to die singly or in groups of two or three. In the long barracks, which had two floors, inevitability took a little longer. There the stairs had to be forced, and a fight in the upper story was added to the bloody fray on the ground floor.

The largest single group of Texians had holed up in a portion of the long barracks which served the garrison as a hospital. How many invaders were wounded gaining admission isn't known, but the fury of the struggle is certified by the forty-two Mexican corpses found outside afterwards. But still the job of clearing the place wasn't done, for a group of Texians at one end of the big room were defying seizure. The attackers found an answer to the problem, however. They dragged in one of the Alamo's captured cannon and blew the cornered men to pieces.

Meanwhile the inner court was also under attack. Its twelve-foot north wall hadn't been tackled, and its southern combination of earthwork and palisade had proved unexpectedly strong. To the east it was protected by the high walls of the chapel—but its weakness was exposed with the taking of the rest of the fort. Only a four-foot wall, and that with a passageway through it, divided it from the plaza.

David Crockett and his Tennesseans, charged with the defense of the court, were trapped in the open for their death fight. Some may have tried to reach the chapel, and one or two may have succeeded before its doors were of necessity barred. Crockett himself, however, evidently attempted to gain the southern barracks but got no farther than the eastern end of it. Unable to attain a haven, he and a few others had huddled together to kill while they could.

Kill they did, too. The world has scarcely seen a more powerful tribe than the first forest-born generation of trans-Appalachian frontiersmen. The Tennesseans bashed, slashed, smashed, crushed, stamped and rent apart the squads upon squads that came at them. Crockett and two of his men were reported to have been found in a heap with seventeen dead Mexicans.

Only the chapel of the Alamo and portions of the barracks where the battle still raged were now in Texian hands. Of all the buildings in the fort the chapel had the thickest and the highest walls. It had, indeed, proved impervious to cannon fire, and for that reason the fort's remaining stock of powder had been stored there. Major Robert Evans, master of ordnance at the Alamo, had been detailed to blow up the magazine if the fort fell, according to Travis' Joe, but he was shot while making a dash for it across the plaza. Therefore the building still stood.

Somehow the men serving the battery in the apse of the chapel had managed to move one of the pieces to its northeast corner, where it commanded the interior of the fort. Loaded with scrap iron, it wrought havoc with the troops massing to storm the chapel doors, though not for very long. One by one the eleven cannoneers were shot down.

When the first attack had commenced, the half-dozen

women and sundry children in the Alamo had been ordered to the comparative safety of the chapel. Of these the only adult North American was Mrs. Almiram Dickenson, who passed on a brief account of what took place in the final phase of the last assault.

Mrs. Dickenson, having a baby at her breast and a husband on the walls, had all there was to worry about. Her first knowledge of total disaster, however, came when Lieutenant Dickenson rushed into the chapel crying: "My God, Sue! the Mexicans are in the fort. If you live, take care of our child!" He then dashed out to die with the rest of the garrison.

The doors of the chapel were barricaded behind him, but within a short while they were battered in by the attackers. A few Texian snipers remained on the roof, but the defenders below were soon overwhelmed. About the last of them was a wounded youngster who managed to reach Mrs. Dickenson's side to ask her to write his family. He had scarcely completed his request when he was killed by a pistol ball.

Having mopped up in the main part of the chapel, some of the Mexicans set about investigating the rest of it. Most of the forward or western portion was still roofed over, sheltering two rooms which flanked the door. To one of these, a chamber which had served the old Mission of San Antonio de Valera as a baptistry, Bowie had been brought. Seguin reported that he had been quartered in the south barracks, but the captain had left on February 29 before the situation became critical. The threat of the assault had made it wise to move the invalid to what safekeeping there was.

It had been hoped that the thick chapel walls would shield him, but it had been foreseen that they might not. He had a brace of loaded pistols with him in addition to the knife which had helped to make his name a byword for cool courage. That courage did not desert him in his last minutes.

There was no one with him except his frightened Negro boy, Ham, but Big Jim Bowie was accustomed to looking after himself. He had one foot and four toes of the other in the grave, but when Mexican soldiers burst open the door he lifted his pistols. He was gasping with pneumonia, and his eyes were glazed with fever, yet he could still use the weapons. He killed two Mexicans and then had to abide their hate. The hand which had once wielded a knife so skillfully was no longer up to it. He was helpless when the bayonets ripped his body.

Who walked off with the great knife as his prize was never known. Nobody took the secret of the wondrous silver mines from him, though. It was lost with his life.

The Mexicans were by then more frenzied than ever. Their own awful casualties, the taste of complete victory over so dangerous an enemy, and the urging of the murderous *deguello* had maddened them until, by the admission of their own officers, they were amok. There were not enough Texians to glut their rage for killing, and many corpses were mutilated. Mrs. Dickenson saw Bowie's body tossed on the bayonets of a dozen soldiers before it was finally thrown to the floor.

Within a few minutes of that bestial incident the remaining snipers had been shot, and the last cornered defenders had been struck down. In all, the three-part assault on the fort took five hours, but the deadly action within the walls is said to have been crammed into thirty minutes. By nine o'clock in the morning of March 6, 1836, the siege of the Alamo was over.

XII

THE PAY-OFF

SANTA ANNA, who had risked his skin in so many battles, did not take an active part in this, the most famous of the encounters with which his name is connected. After the shooting was over he stepped through the gate with a party consisting of some of his staff officers and some Mexican civilians. Among the latter was Francisco Ruiz, alcalde of San Antonio de Bexar, who recorded the event. By his account he was ordered into the Alamo for the specific purpose of identifying for El Presidente the bodies of Travis, Bowie and Crockett.

They were picking their way among the corpses in the plaza when a Mexican officer reported to him with a critically wounded Texian, who had been found hidden in a pile of mattresses in an upper room of the long barracks. The killing fever had passed, the Mexican troops were sated with slaughter, and so the man had been taken prisoner.

Sharply reminding his subordinate that the orders were that no quarter should be given, Santa Anna pointedly turned his back. Several muskets went off, and the last defender of the Alamo died.

Results must be assessed when weighing the worth even of great gallantry. In the case of the Alamo the results matched the heroism which obtained them. The twelve days of grace which the garrison personally gave to the rest of Texas was only a part of the accomplishment. In a word, Santa Anna's army had been so badly mauled that it wasn't able to sweep ahead as planned but had to pause for a complete reorganization of its principal units. This additional enforced delay, it can categorically be stated, was the only thing which saved the North American colonies from being conquered and subjected to the devastating brutality Santa Anna had promised.

The number of Mexicans who were either killed or died from wounds in the course of the siege has been variously estimated; but estimating isn't necessary. Ruiz, to whom was delegated the task of disposing of the corpses, left a statement to the effect that the number of slain Mexicans totaled well over fifteen hundred, "belonging to the flower of the army." This exactly checks with the information obtained by Sutherland. The doctor had recovered from his leg injury by the time of the Battle of San Jacinto and served as a medical officer at that decisive engagement on General Houston's staff. He was present when Santa Anna and members of his staff were being quizzed about the Alamo. Eventually, El Presidente's secretary was asked how many casualties the Mexicans had suffered during the siege. He replied that the dead alone totaled about sixteen hundred. Santa Anna himself, Sutherland pointed out, listened to this statement and by his silence admitted its truth.

There were about sixteen hundred dead, and there must have been a good few wounded, many of them seriously. What's more, most of the casualties were suffered by the pick of Mexican troops, the regulars and the trained militia battalions. One, as has been related, lost over four-fifths of its strength in men killed outright. The other four battalions averaged a loss of 25 per cent, not counting those who were only wounded. These five battalions, forming the body of Santa Anna's force, had to be rebuilt from the squad up. Replacements for officers and non-coms had to be found.

Even though, as Sutherland declared, upwards of a thousand Mexicans from Texas flocked to Santa Anna's standard, the losses were by no means made good. The recruits weren't natural free-lance fighters like the American frontiersmen, and the Mexican army wasn't a collection of independents like that of Texas. It was an organized force into which men could be fitted only after training.

After the Alamo was taken the Mexicans marked time in Bexar for weeks, sending forward only a harrying force under General Sesma. To show just what the delay meant to the cause of Texas independence it is necessary to show just what was going on in the rest of the state.

Houston, it should be remembered, was on leave of absence when the siege began and was improving the time by making a useful treaty with the Cherokees up Red River way. He first heard that the state had been invaded when he was en route to the consultation of delegates at Washington.

If the Alamo hadn't kept Santa Anna at Bexar this consultation, whose purpose was the forming of an effective government, could never have been held. Yet threatened and otherwise defenseless as they were, the delegates took a strong line. Far from being intimidated, they made a declaration of independence and voted into existence the sovereign nation of Texas.

So far, fine, but having made the important primary decisions they bickered endlessly over details. It wasn't until

they learned the Alamo had fallen—six days after the event—
that they finally saw that the only state policy that mattered
at the moment was fighting the war.

Up until then the only constructive step in that direction
had been the reappointment of General Houston as commander in chief. That didn't take place until March 3, the
day Travis dispatched his final message of appeal. The next
day Houston rode west to find out what, if anything, could
be done to help. A commander on paper only, he had but
four men with him.

Meanwhile General Urrea, having snapped up the remnants of the Matamoras Expedition, descended upon Goliad,
where Fannin was still trying to find his mind so that he
could make it up. Confirmed as commander, Houston had
ordered Fannin to withdraw his troops from Goliad, but
Fannin, once again mutinous, refused to move. Then when
it was too late to escape Urrea he decided to obey orders
after all. Abandoning the shelter of Labahia Fortress, he
was run down in the clear by a superior force.

After an indecisive engagement he surrendered, upon, it
is claimed, honorable terms. That meant nothing to Santa
Anna. He sent orders that the prisoners should all be shot;
so on March 26 hundreds of them were taken out to die like
chickens on market day. The original Texian army, the one
which had been so swiftly triumphant in the fall of 1835,
had thus been liquidated by early spring in 1836.

It was the men of the Alamo who put a new army into
Houston's hand. Travis' appeals had not been sent out to
passive men; the Texians had but been waiting for government action to supply them with some sort of leadership.
When none was forthcoming they finally took up arms of
their own volition. Companies and little bands of men
started riding west to the relief of the fortress at Bexar. They

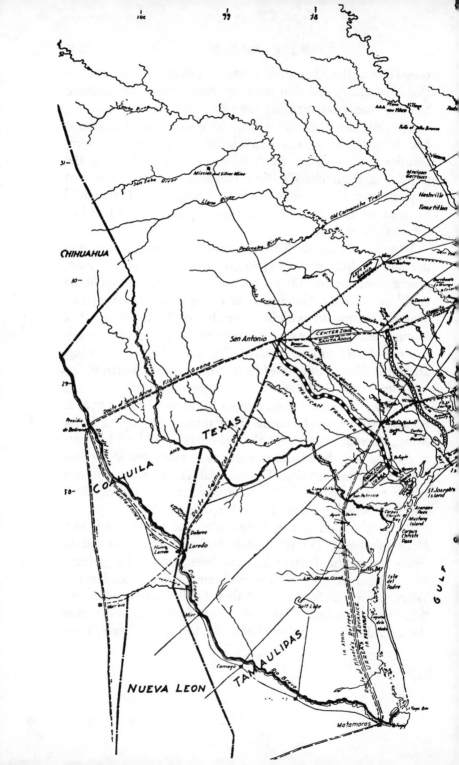

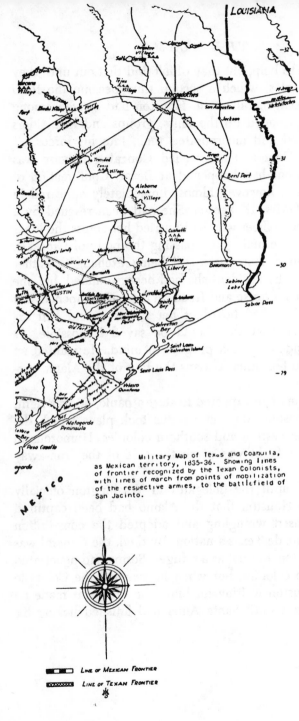

Military Map of Texos and Coahuila, as Mexican territory, 1835-36. Showing lines of frontier recognized by the Texan Colonists, with lines of march from points of mobilization of the respective armies, to the battlefield of San Jacinto.

LINE OF MEXICAN FRONTIER
LINE OF TEXAN FRONTIER

Military Map of Texas, 1835-36. In general this is the best reconstruction available. Most authorities, however, believe Santa Anna crossed the Rio Grande at Laredo and not as shown here.

(This map from *Texas Independence* by Andrew Jackson Houston, copyright 1938, used by permission of the publishers, The Anson Jones Press, Houston, Texas.)

were too late to help, but they didn't find that out until they reached Gonzales, which a second time became the focal point for Texian mobilization. Houston had arrived among the first. He scooped up the units, groups and lone riders as they arrived and incorporated them into his forces.

When the General had reached Gonzales, nobody was certain just what had happened at Bexar. Confirmation of the worst fears, however, almost immediately appeared in the person of Mrs. Dickenson. She had been rescued by a gallant Mexican officer who had hurried her across the inner court and out the main gate—passing the body of Crockett, she noted—while shots were still being exchanged. Either by intention or by accident she had been wounded, but she had been given a horse and freed. What had happened was that Santa Anna had heard of her presence and had expressly ordered that she should be saved if possible. As usual El Presidente had a purpose in mind. He wanted an eye witness to tell other Texians the fate of the Alamo garrison.

If Santa Anna had expected to start a panic, he was right. During the ensuing days an exodus took place which depopulated the western and southern colonies. Humorous in retrospect, this flight was given the title of the "run-away scrape."

It was not until the delegates in Washington officially learned from Houston that the Alamo had been captured that they ceased wrangling and adopted the constitution which really made Texas a nation. By then, the General was heading east, too, but not as a refugee. Sesma had penetrated deep into the colonies, but when he reached the Colorado he found Houston waiting for him. The Mexicans made no further progress until Santa Anna had finished licking his wounds.

To Houston the few weeks of unexpected grace supplied by the siege and its aftermath were the odds of victory. His new army was a coherent force such as the other had never been. The Texians still snarled and beefed at taking orders, but they took them, even when they doubted their wisdom. The need for unity of command had been impressed upon them the hard way.

When Santa Anna finally did get moving he proved that the people who took part in the run-away scrape knew what they were doing. His army moved in multiple columns, burning and confiscating. The old Texian capital of San Felipe de Austin went up in flames, and practically every house south of the Brazos was razed.

Meanwhile, although his troops fumed, Houston made no offensive gesture. He dropped back from the Colorado at Santa Anna's approach, then to the Brazos and afterwards farther still. The outraged Texians, who wanted only to close with the army which was destroying their country, threatened revolt; but Houston somehow kept a tight grip on them while he avoided engagement with the Mexicans time and again.

Finally, near the San Jacinto, the lay of the land was to his liking, and he made a devastating attack. Thus Santa Anna had allowed himself to be drawn into the cardinal blunder of overconfidence. His troops outnumbered the Texians two to one, but they weren't prepared when Houston's men fell upon them. About half were killed, and Santa Anna himself was wounded before he was captured. The battle-cry of the frontiersmen as they rushed from the forest upon the Mexican camp was, "Remember the Alamo!" The phrase was an indirect thanksgiving and a direct pledge to make good use of the opportunity which had been bought

for them by the lives of Travis, Bowie, Crockett, Bonham
and the rest.

The promise was redeemed at San Jacinto, but a strong
force of unconquered Mexicans under General Filisola remained to be dealt with. Additional hostilities were avoided,
however, through Santa Anna's willingness to make every
concession that might further his personal safety. Without
disclosing that he was a prisoner, he sent Filisola orders to
withdraw his troops from Texas.

With Bexar in their hands once more, the Texians were
at last able to find out what disposition had been made of
the Alamo's defenders. They had been stripped and stacked
upon a great funeral pyre; then their charred remains had
been shoveled into a hole. To friends and relatives, believers
in the sacrament of burial, that was a blow; but in his cal-
lous indifference Santa Anna had not done too badly. They
had sacrificed themselves together, and no profit would come
of separating one from the other. They were all men of the
Alamo.

The city of San Antonio spread over the spot where Travis
and his command lay mingled. As the monument which was
later raised could not mark the burial place of the garrison
it was, quite fittingly, placed rather at Austin, the state
capital. There is some question as to how many of the one
hundred and ninety-four names it commemorates justly belong on it. Although several historians believe there were
more, Ruiz, who was in charge of burial operations, made a
count of one hundred and eighty-two. In the absence of
stronger contradictory evidence than is now available, his
figure should stand.

Yet what is or is not inscribed on a stone shaft isn't important. The true monument of the men who died defending
an old mission on March 6, 1836, is the Alamo itself, or

what remains of it. After serving the Texians as a fort and the United States as an arsenal, it ceased to be a military post as it had once ceased to be a religious establishment. Abandoned, it escaped complete decay only by becoming a museum. About all that is left is the ruined chapel.

That, too, may collapse; but the Alamo will remain. The Alamo isn't a structure now; it is a symbol of valor in the minds of men. It can never fall again.

BIBLIOGRAPHY

ALMONTE, JUAN N. "The Private Journal of Juan Nepomuceno Almonte," *Southwestern Historical Quarterly*, Austin: 1944.

ANONYMOUS. *Sketches and Eccentricities of Col. David Crockett of Tennessee*, New York: 1833.

AUSTIN, STEPHEN F. *Three Manuscript Maps of Texas*, edited by Castaneda, Carlos E., and Martin, Early, Jr., Austin: 1930.

BAKER, DEWITT CLINTON. *A Texas Scrapbook*, New York: 1875.

BANCROFT, HUBERT HOWE. *History of the North Mexican States and Texas*, San Francisco: 1889. 2 vols.

BEAZLEY, JULIA. "William Barrett Travis," *Texas Review*, Austin: 1923.

BOATRIGHT, MODY C. (Editor). *From Hell to Breakfast*, Dallas: 1944.

BOLTON, HERBERT EUGENE. *Texas in the Middle Eighteenth Century*, Berkeley: 1915.

———. *With the Makers of Texas*, Austin: 1904.

BROWN, JOHN HENRY. *History of Texas from 1685 to 1892*, St. Louis: 1893. 2 vols.

———. *Indian Wars and Pioneers of Texas*, Austin: 1904.

———. *Life and Times of Henry Smith*, Dallas: 1887.

BUTTERFIELD, JACK C. *Men of the Alamo, Goliad, and San Jacinto*, San Antonio: 1936.

CALLCOTT, WILFRID HARDY. *Santa Anna, the Story of an Enigma Who Once Was Mexico*, Norman: 1936.

CAROLL, MARY TARVER. *The Man Who Would Not Wait,* New York: 1943.

CASTANEDA, CARLOS E. See under Austin, Foik, Morfi, and Santa Anna.

CHABOT, FREDERICK CHARLES. *The Alamo as Mission, Fortress and Shrine,* San Antonio: 1941.

COX, ISAAC JOSLIN. "The Louisiana-Texas Frontier," *Southwest Historical Association Quarterly,* Austin: 1913.

CRANE, OLATIA. *The Guttieres-Magee Expedition,* Austin: 1903.

CROCKETT, DAVID. *A Narrative of the Life of David Crockett, Written by Himself,* Philadelphia: 1834.

DE SHIELDS, JAMES T. *Tall Men with Long Rifles,* San Antonio: 1935.

DIXON, SAMUEL HOUSTON. *Romance and Tragedy of Texas History,* Houston: 1924.

DOBIE, J. FRANK. *Coronado's Children,* New York: 1931.

———. "Bowie and the Bowie Knife," *Southwest Review,* Dallas: 1931.

DOBIE, J. FRANK (Editor). *In the Shadow of History,* Austin: 1939.

DORSON, RICHARD M. *Davy Crockett, American Comic Legend,* New York: 1939.

DOUGLAS, CLAUDE LEROY. *James Bowie: the Life of a Bravo,* Dallas: 1944.

ELLIS, EDWARD S. *Life and Adventures of David Crockett,* New York: 1862.

FIELD, JOSEPH E. *Three Years in Texas,* Boston: 1836.

FOIK, PAUL J. (Editor). *Our Catholic Heritage in Texas* (largely written by Castaneda, Carlos E.), Austin: 1942. 5 vols.

FOOTE, HENRY STUART. *Texas and the Texans,* Philadelphia: 1841. 2 vols.

FORD, JOHN S. *Origin and Fall of the Alamo,* San Antonio: 1896.

GRAY, WILLIAM F. *From Virginia to Texas,* Houston, 1909.

HAY, THOMAS ROBSON. *The Admirable Trumpeter,* Garden City: 1941.

HEISKELL, S. G. *Andrew Jackson and Early Tennessee History,* Nashville: 1918.

HODGE, FREDERICK WEBB. *Handbook of American Indians North of Mexico,* Washington: 1910. 2 vols.

HOLLEY, MARY AUSTIN. *Letters of an Early American Traveler,* Dallas: 1933.

HOUSTON, ANDREW JACKSON. *Texas Independence,* Houston: 1938.

JACOBS, JAMES RIPLEY. *Tarnished Warrior,* New York: 1938.

JAMES, MARQUIS. *The Raven: a Biography of Sam Houston,* Indianapolis: 1924.

———. *They Had Their Hour,* Indianapolis: 1934.

JOHNSON, FRANCIS WHITE. *A History of Texas and Texans,* Chicago: 1914. 2 vols.

JOHNSON, GERALD W. *Andrew Jackson, an Epic in Homespun,* New York: 1927.

KENNEDY, WILLIAM. *Texas, Its Rise, Progress, and Prospects,* London: 1840.

LAMAR, MIRABEAU BUONAPARTE. *The Papers of Mirabeau Buonaparte Lamar,* Austin: 1927. 6 vols.

MAILLARD, N. DORAN. *The History of the Republic of Texas,* Austin: 1842.

MENCHACHA, ANTONIO. *Memoirs,* San Antonio: 1937.

MORFI, JUAN AGUSTIN. *History of Texas* (translated by Castaneda, Carlos E.), Albuquerque: 1935.

MORPHIS, J. M. *History of Texas,* New York: 1875.

NEWELL, CHESTER. *History of the Revolution in Texas,* New York: 1838.

POTTER, REUBEN MARMADUKE. *The Fall of the Alamo,* San Antonio: 1860.

Improved version, Boston: 1904.

ROURKE, CONSTANCE M. *Davy Crockett,* New York: 1934.

SANTA ANNA, ANTONIO LOPEZ DE, and Others. *The Mexican Side of the Texas Revolution* (translated by Castaneda, Carlos E.), Dallas: 1928.

SAXON, LYLE. *Lafitte, the Pirate,* New York: 1930.

SHEA, JOHN GILMARY. *History of the Catholic Missions among the Indian Tribes of the United States,* New York: 1854.

SMITH, RICHARD PENN (Putative author). *Col. Crockett's Exploits and Adventures in Texas,* Philadelphia: 1836.

SOWELL, ANDREW JACKSON. *Rangers and Pioneers of Texas,* San Antonio: 1884.

———. *Early Settlers and Indian Fighters of Southwest Texas,* Austin: 1900.

STIFF, EDWARD. *A New History of Texas*, Cincinnati: 1847.

SUTHERLAND, JOHN. *The Fall of the Alamo*, San Antonio: 1936.

SWISHER, JOHN MILTON. *Journal of John Milton Swisher*, Austin: 1937.

THRALL, HOMER S. *A Pictorial History of Texas*, St. Louis: 1879.

VAN BUREN, MARTIN. *The Autobiography of Martin Van Buren*, Washington: 1920. 2 vols.

WANDELL, SAMUEL HENRY, and MINNIGERODE, MEADE. *Aaron Burr*, New York: 1927. 2 vols.

WARREN, HARRIS GAYLORD. *The Sword Was Their Passport*, Baton Rouge: 1943.

WHITE, DABNEY (Editor). *East Texas, Its History and Its Makers*, New York: 1940. 2 vols.

WILLIAMS, AMELIA. "A Critical Study of the Siege of the Alamo," *Southwestern Historical Quarterly*, Austin: 1934.

WILLIAMS, ROBERT H. "Travis—a Potential Sam Houston," *Southwestern Historical Quarterly*, Austin: 1936.

WOOTEN, DUDLEY GOODALL. *A Comprehensive History of Texas*, Dallas: 1898.

YOAKUM, HENDERSON. *History of Texas from Its First Settlement in 1685 to Its Annexation to the United States in 1846*, New York: 1856. 2 vols.